BEYOND THE NILE

Gods and Legends from the Heart of Africa

Clifton Brown

Clifton Brown

CONTENTS

INTRODUCTION

I n a time when the earth was young, the people of a small West African village gathered under the broad canopy of a baobab tree. The air was thick with anticipation as the village griot, the keeper of stories, began to speak. He wove a tale of Obatala, the god of creation, who descended from the heavens on a golden chain. With the earth beneath him and the sky above, Obatala shaped the first humans from clay, breathing life into their forms. His hands were gentle, his heart full of hope. The people listened, their eyes wide with wonder, as they felt the weight and warmth of their heritage.

This book seeks to capture such stories, these echoes from the past that hold the spirit of whole cultures within them. It is a journey through the pantheons of West, Central, and South Africa, exploring gods and goddesses who have long shaped the lives of their people. Here, I aim to bring to light the myths that have been whispered from one generation to the next, ensuring they are not lost to time.

The vision for this book is to immerse you in these tales, to make you feel as though you are sitting under that ancient tree, hearing the griot's voice. Through detailed stories and careful exploration, I hope to help you understand and appreciate the intricate relationships between these deities and their followers. This work is not just about recounting old tales; it is about reconnecting with a heritage that is rich, diverse, and too often overshadowed by the more widely known Egyptian myths.

Non-Kemetic myths hold a treasure trove of wisdom and insight. While Egyptian mythology often takes center stage, the stories of other African regions are just as vibrant and vital. They offer a window into the diverse cultural heritage of African people, revealing the complexity and depth of their beliefs and traditions.

The structure of this book mirrors the vastness of its subject. We will explore the pantheons of West, Central, and South African deities across several chapters. Each section will delve into the gods and goddesses and their stories. We will also meet mythological creatures, hear fables, and engage in comparative analyses that highlight the similarities and differences across regions.

The geographical diversity and historical events of these regions have shaped their myths. From the lush forests of West Africa to the savannas of Central Africa and the varied landscapes of the South, each locale has left its mark on the stories told by its people. These myths reflect the struggles, triumphs, and moral lessons that have arisen from the rich tapestry of African history.

Oral traditions play a vital role in preserving these stories. Griots, shamans, and storytellers have kept these myths alive through time. Their voices carry the weight of generations, and through them, the myths endure. This book honors their contribution and seeks to continue their work.

On a personal note, my motivation for writing this book stems from a newly found semi-obsession. I began this journey with research for a fiction work I'm writing on a South African mythos surrounding the San People, also known as the oldest continuous population on Earth. Some believe they are directly descended from the First Ones, who descended from a mountaintop to populate the Earth.

When I began my search for non-Kemetic Deities and mythologies, it took more effort than it should. This piqued my interest, so I continued digging. Though I have yet to finish my fiction story, I wanted to present some of my discoveries in this format. While it is nowhere near complete, I've tried to gather enough knowledge in one place so that it may inspire others to continue in more than just an academic fashion.

There is so much about our heritage, our history, that we don't know. We don't have shamans and griots in the United States to pass down the stories from our ancestors because of our displacement, enslavement, and indoctrination. Growing up, I wish I'd known more about our vast, rich, wonderful culture.

We always hear about the Gods from Greek, Egyptian, Norse, Celtic and other mythologies but I have yet to see many books, TV shows or movies about Black African Gods. While this book wont change that, I hope it inspires someone enough to consider it.

Though I've only explored the tip of the iceberg, I wish to help us reconnect with our ancestral roots. I want to bridge the gap that our troubled past has created and offer a path back to cultural heritage. This work is born out of love and respect for the stories that have shaped countless lives.

As you journey through these pages, you'll find narratives that bring to life the gods and goddesses of Africa. You'll gain a basic understanding of their relationships and the roles they play in their respective pantheons. The tales are immersive and rich, offering both entertainment and insight.

Let me be clear: I am not an expert on this topic but a student searching for answers and scratching the surface of a vast world of wonder. I'm excited to share some of my findings with you. Some may say that this book holds a modicum of academic and cultural relevance.

It may serve as a primer for scholars and casual readers alike, offering an introduction to African mythology and cultural studies. May it stand as a testament to the enduring power of these myths and their ability to enlighten and inspire.

However, understand that while stories vary from region to region, I primarily focus on the more favorable interpretations. In addition, this work is simply an introduction to this magnificently varied topic. I hope to drill down on specific details of the different pantheons in future works.

I invite you to embark on this journey with an open heart and mind. Let us explore the rich tapestry of African myths together. These stories hold wisdom and splendor yearning to be uncovered. As you turn the pages, I hope you feel the pull of the past, drawing you closer to a heritage that is vibrant, colorful, and full of life.

One final note, to help you avoid the embarrassment I felt the first time I mispronounced this word when I spoke it out loud, (GREE-oh) is how you say the word Griot. Now that my penance is complete, we may proceed. I pass the responsibility on to all of you.

Ready? The myths are waiting, and the adventure is yours to discover.

CHAPTER I: INTRODUCTION TO NON-KEMETIC AFRICAN MYTHOLOGY

From the standpoint of a Black man growing up in the United States, I never knew anything about the myths and legends from Africa other than the Egyptian Gods. I lost myself in the Greek and Norse Gods I read about in class and comics. I learned about the Celtic, Central, and South American myths and belief systems. I even discovered more about Eastern medicine and mythologies as I searched for ways to calm the rage I found inside me after growing up in a not-so-great neighborhood in 1970's, Houston, Texas.

Much of that information was readily available in local libraries, and I spent much of my time devouring that knowledge in an effort to escape. Neither the elders in my family nor in my church ever spoke of our African origins. I matured, never knowing what an amazingly rich, vibrant culture I came from. I do now, and I wish to share what little I've learned so far.

I'm sure there are many others who know our heritage much better than I do. I admit that I'm a novice, but during my search for more information, I discovered a distinct lack of it without digging deeply. Though I'm only scratching the surface of the mountain of information available, follow me on this journey.

There was a time when, under the vast African sky, the people of different tribes would sit around the fire, their faces painted with the glow of dancing flames. They would listen as the village griot spoke, his voice weaving tales of gods and goddesses. These stories weren't just for entertainment; they were the lifeblood of the community, passing down wisdom, history, and cultural identity from one generation to the next.

When we think of African mythology, the tales of Egyptian gods like Ra and Isis might come to mind first. These are the stories that books and movies often spotlighted, overshadowing the rich tapestry of mythologies from other parts of Africa. But beyond the pyramids and the Nile lies a world of stories that are just as vibrant, filled with gods and goddesses who reflect the diverse cultures of the continent's interior. This chapter is about those stories—the myths that have shaped the lives and beliefs of people across West, Central, and Southern Africa.

THE DISTINCTION FROM KEMETIC (EGYPTIAN) MYTHOLOGY

Kemetic mythology, centered around the grandeur of pharaohs and monumental structures, presents a world where the state and religion are deeply intertwined. The pharaohs, seen as gods on earth, were the central figures in a narrative where state and divine power were one and the same. Temples and pyramids stood as testaments to their reign, with Ra, the sun god, embodying the cycle of life and death. These stories speak of order and cosmic balance, reflecting a civilization that held the sun and its cycles in reverence.

In stark contrast, Non-Kemetic African mythologies offer a kaleidoscope of narratives that mirror the diverse cultural landscapes they arise from. Here, you won't find the towering pyramids or grand temples; instead, these myths thrive in the oral traditions of diverse tribes, each with its own pantheon of deities. The gods and goddesses of these regions are as varied as the landscapes they inhabit, from the savannas of the Sahel to the dense forests of the Congo. Each tribe brings its own flavor to the myths, with beliefs shaped by the land they call home.

The environments of these regions play a significant role in shaping their mythologies. In West Africa, the sprawling savannas and lush rainforests influence tales where nature often takes center stage. Gods like Olodumare, the supreme deity of the Yoruba, oversee the balance of life, much like Ra, yet in a context deeply connected to the earth and its cycles. In the coastal regions, deities like Mami Wata hold dominion over the waters, embodying both beauty and danger, unlike the more serene Isis of the Nile.

The storytelling methods themselves differ greatly. While Kemetic myths often follow a linear progression, non-Kemetic myths embrace a cyclical narrative, reflecting the ongoing cycle of life and nature. Animals frequently play pivotal roles, symbolizing various virtues and vices. This is seen in tales of Shango, the god of thunder, whose fiery nature mirrors the storms that sweep across the African plains, a stark contrast to the more rigid Egyptian god Set. These myths have been preserved through oral traditions, passed down by griots and shamans, ensuring their survival across generations despite the absence of written records.

Let's explore a few examples to paint a clearer picture of these distinctions. Consider Olodumare and Ra: both are creators, yet Olodumare's narrative is deeply interwoven with the earth and its elements, reflecting the Yoruba's connection to their land. Shango, a god of chaos and order, stands in contrast to Set, whose narrative is often one of villainy and discord within the ordered universe of Egyptian lore. Mami Wata, with her fluidity and mystique, dances differently in the waters than Isis, whose legacy is rooted in the calm, fertile banks of the Nile.

These stories, while diverse, share a common thread—they are the voices of the ancestors, speaking across time to remind us of who we are and where we come from. Through them, we see the reflection of African cultures, each unique yet connected by the shared human experience.

THE IMPORTANCE OF NON-KEMETIC MYTHOLOGIES IN AFRICAN CULTURES

Imagine sitting around a fire, the night sky vast and endless above you, as a storyteller begins to speak. In many African cultures, mythologies serve as more than just tales of gods and heroes; they are the very fabric of cultural identity and heritage. Myths explain the unexplainable, providing reasons for natural phenomena and guiding moral conduct. When a sudden storm would sweep across a village, it wasn't just the weather; it was Shango, the god of thunder, expressing his power. These stories taught communities about the world and their place within it, grounding them in a shared understanding of life's mysteries.

The social functions of these myths extend beyond mere explanations. They teach moral lessons and establish societal norms, reflecting the values held dear by each community. When elders told stories of Anansi the spider, they weren't just entertaining the young ones; they were imparting wisdom about cunning and resourcefulness, illustrating the virtues of intelligence over brute strength. Such tales became living textbooks, shaping the ethical foundations of entire societies. They preserved historical events, embedding them in the cultural consciousness so that even when the details faded, the essence remained alive and relevant.

African myths weave themselves into the daily life of communities, influencing everything from rituals to festivals. Consider the vibrant harvest festivals that honor fertility deities, celebrating the bounty of the earth and the gods' blessings. These events are not just about the crops; they're about community, gratitude, and the acknowledgment of divine influence. Rites of passage, too, often draw from mythological underpinnings, marking transitions in life with ceremonies that honor the gods and ancestors. These rituals reaffirm connections to the past, guiding individuals as they step into new roles within the tribe. Mythological stories, whether told around a fire or through dance and music, permeate cultural practices, ensuring that they are lived experiences rather than distant memories.

The impact of these myths is not confined to the past. Their influence echoes through modern African and African-American cultures, seen in literature, art, and spiritual practices. Writers draw on mythological themes to explore identity and resilience, while artists incorporate symbols and narratives into their work, creating a dialogue between the past and present. Spiritual practices, too, reflect these enduring myths, with rituals and beliefs adapted to fit contemporary contexts. Even in music and film, mythological themes resonate, offering powerful narratives that connect people across time and space. The myths offer a rich tapestry of stories and ideas, providing a cultural backbone that supports and inspires.

Despite the pressures of colonization and globalization, these traditions have shown remarkable resilience. Oral transmission plays a pivotal role in their survival, with stories passed from one generation to the next, adapting as needed without losing their essence. This flexibility allows myths to remain relevant, evolving with the communities they belong to. In a world where written records can be lost or distorted, the spoken word becomes a powerful tool for preservation. Even as new contexts emerge, the core elements of these myths endure, speaking to the strength and adaptability of African cultural traditions.

As we explore these mythologies, we see their power not only in the stories themselves but in their role as living, breathing elements of cultural identity. They connect the past to the present, offering wisdom and insight that transcend time. These myths are not relics of a bygone era; they are vibrant, dynamic forces that continue to shape the lives and identities of those who embrace them. Their significance lies in their ability to teach, guide, and inspire, making them an integral part of the cultural landscape.

CULTURAL AND HISTORICAL CONTEXT OF AFRICAN MYTHOLOGIES

To genuinely appreciate African mythologies, we must consider the historical and cultural landscapes from which they emerged. Picture the bustling markets of the Mali Empire, where traders and travelers exchanged not only goods but also stories and beliefs. Pre-colonial kingdoms across Africa thrived, each with its own heroes and legends. These myths served as a reflection of societal values and historical events. For instance, the founding of the Mali Empire is intertwined with the epic of Sundiata Keita in the 13th century C.E. He was its legendary first ruler whose story speaks of resilience, destiny, and divine favor. These tales offered a sense of identity and continuity in a world where change was constant.

Trade and migration played pivotal roles in the exchange of mythologies across different regions. As people moved, so did their stories, evolving and adapting to new cultural contexts. Caravan routes crisscrossed the Sahara, connecting distant lands and facilitating the spread of ideas and beliefs. This exchange enriched the mythologies, creating a tapestry of narratives that reflected the diverse influences and interactions between tribes and nations. For instance, the god Eshu, a trickster figure in Yoruba mythology, found parallels in other African cultures, highlighting the shared themes and archetypes that transcend geographical boundaries.

Historical events often found their echoes in mythological narratives. Consider the tales of divine intervention in battles, where gods and goddesses were said to have influenced the outcomes of conflicts. These stories not only glorified the past but also served to legitimize the rule of kings and chiefs. The mythological narratives provided a divine seal of approval, reinforcing the authority and legitimacy of rulers. In the Kingdom of Dahomey, for example, the king traced his lineage back to the gods, establishing a connection between the divine and the earthly realm. Such stories were integral to governance and law, forming the foundation of political and legal systems.

Mythology played a crucial role in governance, shaping the very fabric of society. Divine kingship, a concept where rulers were seen as descendants or representatives of the gods, was common in many African kingdoms. This belief system not only legitimized their rule but also established them as mediators between the gods and their people. Laws and societal standards often drew from mythological narratives, providing a moral and ethical framework for communities.

The stories of Queen Nzinga, for instance, illustrate how mythology justified her reign and her resistance against colonial powers, portraying her as a warrior queen guided by divine wisdom and strength. Even in her sixties, she spearheaded guerilla attacks against the Portuguese slave trade, who failed to capture or kill her. She was in her eighties when she died peacefully in 1663.

These mythologies, though steeped in the past, resonate with historical figures and events that have shaped African societies. They offer a bridge between history and myth, blending fact with fiction to create narratives that inform and inspire. By exploring these stories, we gain insight into the cultural and historical context of African societies, understanding how myths have influenced politics, law, and societal norms. These narratives are not just relics of the past; they are living stories that continue to shape the identities and values of African people, both on the continent and in the diaspora. Through them, we glimpse the enduring legacy of African cultures, rich in tradition and resilience, and their impact on the world today.

THE ROLE OF ORAL TRADITIONS IN PRESERVING MYTHS

The heart of African mythology beats strongest in the oral traditions that have carried stories through countless generations. Imagine a time when the night sky served as a backdrop to tales that danced from the tongues of griots and storytellers, the revered guardians of history. In West African societies, griots, also known as jali or gewel, were more than entertainers; they were the custodians of cultural memory. Their role was to preserve genealogies, historical narratives, and the rich tapestry of myths that defined a community's identity. With the kora, a 21-stringed harp-lute, they wove music with words, creating a living archive that was shared and remembered.

Oral storytelling is a craft, one that demands precision and creativity. Storytellers employ various techniques to ensure the accuracy and consistency of each tale. Repetition plays a vital role, embedding the narrative deep into the memory of both the teller and the listener. A griot might repeat a verse or a phrase, allowing it to resonate, much like a refrain in a song. Through this method, the story becomes not just a tale, but a shared experience. Additionally, vivid imagery and metaphor transform abstract ideas into tangible images that listeners can easily grasp and retain. This vividness ensures that even as stories travel across generations, their core essence remains intact.

Despite the strengths of oral traditions, challenges persist. The risk of alteration looms over each retelling, as personal interpretations might lead to subtle shifts in detail. Over generations, these changes can accumulate, potentially altering the myth's original message. Yet, this very risk is also a testament to the flexibility and adaptability of oral traditions. As societies evolve, so too do their stories, adapting to new contexts while preserving their foundational truths. This adaptability allows myths to remain relevant, speaking to the present while echoing the past.

Among the most significant contributors to this legacy are the griot families, whose lineage of storytellers has kept traditions alive through centuries. These families often pass down their roles from one generation to the next, ensuring continuity and preserving the integrity of the myths. Renowned storytellers, such as Amadou Kouyaté, have become legends in their own right, celebrated for their masterful renditions of age-old tales. Through their dedication, the stories endure, bridging the gap between past and present.

In recent times, there has been a resurgence of interest in these oral traditions, spurred by cultural movements that seek to reclaim and celebrate African heritage. Across the continent and the diaspora, festivals dedicated to traditional storytelling have emerged, offering a platform for griots and storytellers to share their craft with new audiences. These gatherings are more than mere entertainment; they are a reaffirmation of identity and cultural pride.

For instance, The National Black Storytelling Festival and Conference, promoted by the National Association of Black Storytellers (NABS), occurs every year, usually in a different city.

I must also mention Sona Jobarteh, a woman born into one of the five primary Griot families of West Africa. Their combined histories date back to the Mali empire. She is the first woman known to have mastered the Kora and has taken up the mantle as a living archive of the Gambian people. While rare, it is not unknown.

The craft of the griot is called Jaliyaa. When women perform the duties, they are known as Jalimuso or Jelimuso, depending on which region you enter, with muso meaning woman. The craft is usually passed from father to son and mother to daughter.

The digital age has also opened new avenues for preserving and disseminating these myths. Platforms like YouTube and podcasts allow griots to reach a global audience, ensuring that their stories are heard far beyond their local communities. This digital preservation not only safeguards these narratives against the erosion of time but also allows them to flourish in new and unexpected ways. By recording these myths, we create a digital archive that future generations can access, keeping the spirit of the griot alive in the modern world.

As we conclude this exploration, it's clear that oral traditions are the lifeblood of African mythology. They are the threads that weave together the past, present, and future, ensuring that the stories of the gods and goddesses continue to inspire and educate. These myths are not just tales of old; they are living legacies that connect us to our roots, reminding us of the power of storytelling and the resilience of culture. Through the voices of the griots and the melodies of the kora, these stories live on, vibrant and enduring, waiting to be heard.

CHAPTER 2: WEST AFRICAN PANTHEON

Picture this: a vast, starry night sky stretching endlessly over a Yoruba village. The air is alive with the sound of drums, their rhythm steady and grounding. Elders gather under the ancient iroko tree, their voices weaving tales as old as time itself. Tonight, they speak of Olodumare, the supreme creator, the god whose presence is felt in every leaf, every breath, every heartbeat. Olodumare is not just a name; he is the pulse of the universe, the unseen force that holds everything together. The Yoruba people believe that before the world was formed, there was only darkness and silence. It was Olodumare who spoke the first words of creation, bringing the universe into being. With a thought, he ignited the stars, laid the earth's foundation, and set the cosmos in motion. Yet, despite his omnipotence, Olodumare chose not to rule alone. Instead, he entrusted the Orishas, a group of powerful deities, with the task of managing the world. Each Orisha was given a specific domain, from the sea to the skies, allowing the divine to touch every aspect of existence.

Olodumare's role as the creator and supreme deity is central in Yoruba cosmology, where he is the ultimate source of life and existence. His creation of the universe is a testament to his boundless power and wisdom. In the Yoruba creation myth,

Olodumare appointed Olorun, his eldest son, to lay the foundation of the universe. This act of delegation reflects the Yoruba values of cooperation and harmony, emphasizing the importance of community and collective goals. The Orishas, who serve as intermediaries between humans and Olodumare, provide wisdom, guidance, and protection, embodying the diverse forces of nature and the human experience.

In Yoruba art and culture, Olodumare is often represented through symbols of purity and omnipotence. The color white, a representation of his purity, is frequently used in religious ceremonies and rituals to honor him. This color symbolizes cleanliness, peace, and the divine, reflecting his exalted status. In Yoruba culture, white is the color of the sacred, worn by priests and priestesses during religious ceremonies to signify their connection to Olodumare. Artistic depictions of Olodumare are rare, as his presence is considered too vast and encompassing to be captured in a single image. Instead, the focus is on the symbols and rituals that honor his essence.

The influence of Olodumare on Yoruba religion and practices is profound. Priests and priestesses play a vital role in worship, acting as conduits between the divine and the earthly realm. Rituals and offerings dedicated to Olodumare are central to Yoruba religious life, serving as expressions of devotion and reverence. These ceremonies often involve music, dance, and the sharing of food, creating a communal experience that strengthens bonds between participants. Annual festivals and celebrations honor Olodumare's contributions to the community, providing opportunities for reflection and renewal. These events are marked by joy and gratitude, as people come together to acknowledge the blessings bestowed by the supreme deity.

In myths and stories, Olodumare's significance is highlighted through his decisions and interactions with humanity. One such story tells of the creation of the earth, where Olodumare sent Obatala, the Orisha of creation, to shape the world and its inhabitants. This myth underscores Olodumare's role as the architect of existence, setting the stage for the unfolding of life. Another tale explains Olodumare's decision to remain distant from daily affairs, entrusting the Orishas with the care of the world. This distance reflects his wisdom, allowing the divine forces to work in harmony and balance. Through these stories, Olodumare's presence is felt, his influence shaping the lives and destinies of the Yoruba people.

Reflection Section: Exploring Your Connection

As you learn about Olodumare's role and significance, take a moment to reflect on your own understanding of creation and the divine. Consider how these myths resonate with your beliefs and experiences. How do they connect you to your roots and cultural heritage? If you wish, take a moment to write down your thoughts and insights, exploring the ways in which these stories enrich your understanding of the world and your place within it.

SHANGO: THE GOD OF THUNDER AND LIGHTNING

In the heart of Yoruba mythology, Shango stands as a formidable figure, the god whose roar is heard in every clap of thunder and whose fury ignites the sky with lightning. Known for his fiery temper and indomitable warrior spirit, Shango embodies both the destructive power of nature and the righteous fury of justice. His presence is felt in the storm's rage and the crackle of fire. The symbols associated with Shango are as powerful as the deity himself. The double-headed axe, or oshe, is his emblem, representing his ability to strike down foes and deliver swift justice. This axe is not just a weapon; it is a symbol of balance, reminding us that power must be wielded wisely. In rituals, the beat of the drums and the energy of dance are integral to Shango's worship. The drums echo his thunder, while the dancers mimic the lightning's wild, unpredictable path across the sky. Together, they create a sacred space where the divine touches the earthly, and Shango's spirit is invoked.

Shango's rise to divinity is a story steeped in both history and myth and tragedy. Before he was a god, Shango was a king in the Yoruba town of Oyo. His reign was marked by strength and charisma, but also by controversy. Legend tells of a challenge to his rule, a moment of crisis that led Shango to retreat to the wilderness. It was here that the myth of his self-immolation unfolds. Consumed by despair, Shango took his own life, but this act was not the end. His followers believe he ascended to the heavens and transformed into an Orisha, a powerful deity whose spirit continued to guide and protect his people. This transformation from king to god elevated Shango to a place of reverence and worship, where he was venerated for his strength, courage, and unyielding spirit.

Shango's influence extends beyond his control over the elements. In matters of justice and warfare, he is a divine judge, a protector of warriors and soldiers. Many myths describe Shango presiding over disputes, delivering verdicts with a fairness that reflects his understanding of both human nature and divine law. His role as a patron of warriors is equally significant, as he is said to bestow strength and courage upon those who fight in his name. In battle, Shango's presence is a source of inspiration, a reminder that justice and valor are intertwined. His protection extends to those who uphold these values, ensuring victory for the righteous.

The relationships Shango maintains with other Orishas are as dynamic as the storms he commands. His rivalry with Ogun, the god of iron, is a tale of competition and respect, where both deities represent different aspects of strength and power. While Shango is the embodiment of fire and lightning, Ogun's domain is the earth and its minerals, creating a balance between the forces of nature.

Shango's marriages to goddesses like Oba, Oya, and Oshun add complexity to his narrative. Oba was his first wife and goddess of the Oba River. Oya, the goddess of wind and storms, complements Shango's fiery nature, while Oshun, the goddess of love and fertility, offers a softer, more nurturing connection. These relationships highlight the interconnectedness of the divine, where alliances and rivalries shape the cosmos.

For those who follow Shango, his story is one of transformation and resilience. His followers see in him a reflection of human struggles and triumphs, a god who understands the complexities of life and the challenges of leadership. Through worship and devotion, they seek his guidance, drawing strength from his example. Shango's narrative is a reminder of the power that lies within each of us to overcome adversity and embrace the divine potential in our lives.

OSHUN: THE GODDESS OF LOVE AND FERTILITY

Imagine standing by a river, its waters shimmering under the sun's embrace, reflecting the energy and allure of Oshun, also known as Osun. As the goddess of love, fertility, and freshwater, Oshun's presence is felt in the gentle flow of rivers and the nurturing embrace of water bodies. Her essence speaks to the beauty and femininity that water embodies. Oshun is a symbol of grace and abundance, often associated with the richness of gold and the sweetness of honey. These elements play a significant role in her worship, representing prosperity and the sweetness of life. Gold, with its radiant luster, mirrors Oshun's divine beauty, while honey, with its golden hue and sweet taste, signifies Oshun's nurturing spirit and the joy she brings to the world.

Oshun's arrival on earth is a story that resonates with the power of renewal and hope. Sent by Olodumare with other Orishas to populate the earth, Oshun's gifts to humanity were manifold. When the male Orishas failed to revive the barren land, it was Oshun who poured her powerful waters over the earth, breathing life into it. Her waters did not just quench the parched soil; they brought fertility and abundance, ensuring the survival of future generations. This myth underscores Oshun's vital role in creation and her deep connection to the cycles of life and rebirth. Throughout the ages, Oshun's interventions in human affairs through love and fertility have been celebrated in countless stories. Her compassion and wisdom often guide her devotees, helping them navigate the complexities of love, relationships, and family. In the creation of the Ifa divination system, Oshun's influence is particularly notable. She is credited with providing the spiritual insight necessary for the system, which continues to guide and enlighten the Yoruba people.

The veneration of Oshun is a vibrant expression of faith and gratitude, particularly during the annual Osun festival at the Osun-Osogbo Sacred Grove. This event is a time of celebration, reflection, and renewal, drawing devotees from far and wide to pay homage to the goddess. Rituals involving offerings of sweet foods and fresh water are central to these celebrations, symbolizing the abundance and vitality that Oshun bestows upon her followers. Participants gather by the river, adorned in bright colors, singing songs of praise and gratitude. The air is filled with the scent of flowers and incense, creating a sacred atmosphere where the divine and earthly realms converge. These rituals are not just about honoring Oshun; they are about reaffirming the bonds between individuals and their communities, fostering a sense of unity and shared purpose.

Oshun's relationships with other deities and humans further highlight her influence and importance. Her marriage to Shango, the god of thunder, is a testament to her ability to balance passion with harmony. Oshun's romantic entanglements reflect her complex and multifaceted nature, embodying the full spectrum of human emotions. These relationships are depicted in myths where Oshun's compassion and assistance to her devotees are celebrated. She is often portrayed as a mediator, a voice of reason and understanding in times of conflict. Her empathy and nurturing spirit touch the lives of those who seek her guidance, offering solace and support in times of need. Oshun's influence extends beyond the divine realm, impacting the lives of her followers in profound and meaningful ways.

In the vast tapestry of Yoruba mythology, Oshun stands as a beacon of hope, love, and life. Her stories are not just tales of the past; they are living narratives that continue to inspire and guide those who honor her. Oshun's presence is a reminder of the beauty and power that lies within each of us, urging us to embrace the fullness of life with open hearts and minds. As you explore the myths and rituals associated with Oshun, may you find your own connection to the divine, and may her spirit illuminate your path.

ESHU: THE TRICKSTER AND MESSENGER GOD

Among the Yoruba deities, Eshu stands out as a figure of duality and complexity, embodying both the unpredictability of a trickster and the dependability of a messenger. Imagine a crossroads at dusk, where paths intersect and decisions must be made; this is the realm of Eshu, the master of choices and chaos. As a trickster, Eshu delights in stirring the pot, creating situations that challenge individuals and societies. His actions, while seemingly mischievous, often serve a greater purpose, testing the integrity and resilience of those he encounters. Eshu's role as a divine messenger is equally crucial; he bridges the gap between the gods and humanity, ensuring communication flows smoothly. In this capacity, Eshu is a facilitator, a negotiator who moves between worlds with ease, carrying messages and offerings from humans to the divine realm and back again.

Eshu's stories are as varied as they are intriguing, each one a testament to his cunning and wisdom. One famous tale recounts how Eshu created discord in a village by wearing a hat that was red on one side and black on the other. As he walked down the village path, some villagers saw the red side, while others saw the black, leading to a heated argument over what color the hat indeed was. Eshu's lesson? Perspective matters, and sometimes, conflicts arise from simple misunderstandings. Another story tells of Eshu's participation in the redistribution of the world's languages, where his cleverness ensured that communication would always be a challenge, a puzzle to be solved. Through these narratives, Eshu invites us to question our assumptions and embrace the complexity of life.

In Yoruba art and iconography, Eshu is often depicted at the crossroads, a symbol of choice and destiny. Crossroads hold special significance in Eshu's mythology, representing the intersection of possibilities and the point at which paths diverge. Here, Eshu stands as a guardian, a guide who can either aid or obstruct, depending on his whims. The colors red and black are closely associated with Eshu, symbolizing his dual nature and the balance between order and chaos. These colors adorn the altars and offerings made in his honor, a testament to his multifaceted character. In artistic representations, Eshu is often shown with a mischievous smile, a reminder of his playful yet profound influence on the world.

Eshu's presence is deeply ingrained in Yoruba daily life and rituals, where his influence is both respected and revered. In the practice of Ifa divination, Eshu plays a pivotal role as the opener of ways, the one who clears the path for communication with the divine. Diviners call upon Eshu to bless their endeavors, ensuring that the insights they seek are revealed clearly and truthfully. Rituals and offerings to appease Eshu are a common aspect of Yoruba religious practices. These acts of devotion are meant to honor Eshu's power and seek his favor, acknowledging his ability to both aid and challenge. Participants might offer kola nuts, palm oil, or other symbolic items, each chosen for its significance in Eshu's mythology. Through these rituals, the Yoruba people maintain a dynamic relationship with Eshu, one that is ever-evolving and deeply personal.

In weaving the tales of Eshu, we find a deity who embodies the complexities of life, a figure who challenges us to think deeply and act wisely. Eshu's stories remind us that while life may be unpredictable, it is also rich with opportunities for growth and understanding. His presence at the crossroads invites us to consider our choices and embrace the possibilities that lie ahead. As we reflect on Eshu's role in Yoruba mythology, we see a mirror held up to our own lives, a reminder that the path we choose is ours to define.

CHAPTER 3: CENTRAL AFRICAN PANTHEON

Picture, if you will, a vast expanse of sky that seems to go on forever in an unbroken blanket of blue. The sun's warm glow touches every corner of the earth, beckoning you to step outside and bask in its embrace.

In the heart of the Kongo, this vast expanse is not just a backdrop but a divine presence, embodied by Nzambi a Mpungu, the Supreme Creator God. Known as the Sky Father and God of the Sun, Nzambi a Mpungu holds a revered place in Kongo spirituality. His influence is felt in the gentle caress of the morning sun and the vibrant life it nurtures. As the ultimate deity, Nzambi a Mpungu is the architect of creation, the force behind the world and all its inhabitants. He is the one who brought forth the earth from the chaos of the cosmos, shaping the mountains, rivers, and the very air we breathe. Yet, despite his boundless power, he is not a solitary figure. In his wisdom, Nzambi a Mpungu delegated tasks to other spirits and deities, each entrusted with a piece of the cosmic puzzle. This delegation reflects the interconnectedness of all things, reminding us that even the divine must collaborate to maintain harmony.

Nzambi a Mpungu's attributes are as vast as the sky he governs. Omnipotence and benevolence are woven into the fabric of his being, embodying the duality of strength and kindness. He is both the mighty protector and the gentle nurturer, a god whose presence is a source of comfort and inspiration. In Kongo art and religious artifacts, Nzambi a Mpungu is often depicted with symbols that reflect his divine nature. The sun, a powerful emblem of life and renewal, is a common motif, representing his role as the giver of light and warmth. Fire, too, is associated with Nzambi a Mpungu, symbolizing change and transformation. This element speaks to his ability to renew and revitalize, to burn away the old and make way for the new. These symbols are not mere decorations; they are a testament to Nzambi a Mpungu's enduring influence and the reverence he commands.

In Kongo religion and practices, Nzambi a Mpungu's presence is felt in the rituals and ceremonies that honor him. Priests and ritual leaders play a crucial role in facilitating this connection, acting as intermediaries between the divine and the earthly realm. Their chants and prayers reach out to Nzambi a Mpungu, seeking his guidance and blessing. Common rituals include offerings of food, drink, and other symbolic items, each chosen for its significance in Kongo spirituality. These offerings are a gesture of gratitude, a way for the community to express their appreciation for the gifts bestowed upon them. The rituals are often accompanied by music and dance, creating a vibrant celebration of life and faith. Through these practices, Nzambi a Mpungu is not just a distant deity; he is a beloved guardian, a part of the community's daily life.

Nzambi a Mpungu's significance is also reflected in the myths and stories that have been passed down through generations. One such tale speaks of the creation of the first humans, a story that highlights Nzambi a Mpungu's role as the life-giver. In this myth, he is portrayed as a compassionate creator, crafting humans with care and intention. His hands molded the clay, shaping each person with unique features and qualities. Another myth tells of Nzambi a Mpungu's interventions in human affairs, where his wisdom and foresight guide his people through challenges and conflicts. These stories serve as a reminder of Nzambi a Mpungu's enduring presence and his commitment to the well-being of his creation.

During my search for knowledge, I came across a Master's thesis written in 2022 by Anthony Baxter Jr. as part of his requirements for his degree at the University of Florida. If you'd like a more in-depth study on how vital Nzambi a Mpungu is to the Kongo, I would suggest reading this paper. It is fascinating. The title of the paper is: THE HAND OF NZAMBI: AN ETHNOGRAPHIC STUDY OF PALO MAYOMBE NKISI MALONGO ACROSS THE ATLANTIC. You can find the link in the references section.

Reflection Section: Your Connection to Nzambi a Mpungu

As you explore Nzambi a Mpungu's role and significance, take a moment to reflect on your own understanding of creation and divinity. Consider how these myths resonate with your beliefs and experiences. How do they connect you to your roots and cultural heritage? Use this space to jot down your thoughts and insights, exploring the ways in which these stories enrich your understanding of the world and your place within it.

SIMBI: THE WATER SPIRITS AND GUARDIANS

When you think of water, you might imagine rivers flowing effortlessly or the gentle lapping of waves. In Central African mythology, these images come alive through the presence of the Simbi, the revered water spirits and guardians. They are not a single entity but a collection of lesser deities who hold dominion over several facets of Kongo belief systems. While some watch over the lands and forests, pathways and travel, others are considered to be revered ancestors who have a strong connection to the physical world. However, they are also tied closely to water.

Simbi holds dominion over water bodies, from the smallest streams to the vastness of the mighty Congo River. Their presence is a reminder of water's life-giving properties and its potential to both nurture and destroy. The Simbi spirits are protectors, watching over communities and ensuring the balance of nature. They are believed to control the rhythms of aquatic life, governing the ebb and flow of tides and the fertility of the land they touch. Simbi's guardianship extends to safeguarding the resources that sustain life, ensuring that water remains a source of sustenance and prosperity. Their influence is felt in the gentle rains that nourish crops and the rivers that provide sustenance to villages.

Stories of Simbi's benevolence and power have been passed down through generations, each tale a testament to their enduring presence. One such legend speaks of the healing waters of Simbi, where ailing villagers would journey to seek relief from their ailments. It is said that the waters, blessed by Simbi, possessed the ability to cleanse and heal, restoring health and vitality to those in need. This myth illustrates Simbi's role as a healer, a benevolent force that brings solace and hope to the afflicted. Another tale recounts Simbi's assistance in agricultural prosperity, where the spirits guided farmers in harnessing the power of water to irrigate their fields. Through their guidance, crops flourished, and harvests were bountiful, ensuring the well-being of the community. Simbi's guidance also extends to those who navigate the waters, such as fishermen and travelers. They are said to bless those who respect the natural world, offering protection and safe passage across treacherous waters. These stories are more than folklore; they are lessons in respect and harmony with nature.

Simbi is deeply embedded in Central African art and iconography, their presence reflected in the symbols and objects that celebrate their role. Water and aquatic animals, such as fish and serpents, are potent symbols in Simbi's mythology, representing the fluidity and mystery of the natural world. These elements are often depicted in art, serving as reminders of Simbi's omnipresence and influence. In various artistic expressions, Simbi may be portrayed with features of both human and animal, embodying the connection between land and water. This duality speaks to their ability to traverse both realms, acting as intermediaries between the physical and spiritual worlds. Visual representations of Simbi often capture the essence of water's beauty and power, using flowing lines and vibrant colors to convey the dynamic nature of the spirits.

The rituals and practices associated with Simbi are vibrant expressions of faith and gratitude, reflecting the community's reverence for these water spirits. Rituals often involve offerings of water and aquatic plants, symbolic gestures that honor Simbi's guardianship and seek their blessing. These offerings are typically made at sacred sites, such as natural springs or riverbanks, where the presence of Simbi is believed to be strongest. Annual festivals celebrate Simbi's influence, bringing together communities in joyful celebration. During these events, participants engage in music and dance, invoking the spirits through rhythm and movement. These festivals are not only a time of worship but also of reflection and renewal, where individuals reaffirm their connection to the natural world and the spirits that guide them. Through these practices, the relationship between humans and Simbi is strengthened, ensuring that the balance of nature is maintained and respected.

KIMPA VITA: THE PROPHETESS AND HER INFLUENCE

Not all those who found or influenced belief systems were deities. Some mortals have been deified, while others inspired both myths and legends through their transformative deeds. These select few have saved their people by preventing outside influences from diluting their historical legacy and restoring their faith in the traditions their ancestors held dear.

In the late 17th century, amidst the turmoil and upheaval in the kingdom of Kongo, a young woman named Kimpa Vita emerged as a beacon of hope and spiritual insight. Born into a noble family, Kimpa Vita was not just a healer but a visionary, known for her profound spiritual messages and charismatic presence. Her visions spoke of unity and renewal, daring to challenge the existing religious order by merging traditional African spiritual practices with elements of Christianity. Kimpa Vita's influence extended beyond her immediate community. She became a catalyst for religious reform, boldly proclaiming herself the reincarnation of St. Anthony. Her teachings centered on the belief that Jesus was born in Kongo, a radical idea that sought to empower her people and reframe their spiritual narrative. Through her words, Kimpa Vita sought to restore the kingdom of Kongo to its former glory, advocating for a syncretic form of Christianity that embraced African cultural identity. Her message resonated deeply with those who longed for change, making her a pivotal figure in the spiritual landscape of Kongo.

Kimpa Vita's legacy is built on courage and spiritual leadership. She was a trailblazer whose actions inspired both reverence and controversy. Her bold stance against colonial powers and their imposed religious doctrines marked her as both a spiritual leader and a political force. Modern Kongo religious movements view Kimpa Vita as a symbol of resilience and empowerment, her story serving as a reminder of the power of faith and conviction. Her influence is evident in contemporary Kongo spirituality, where she is celebrated as a pioneer who dared to forge a path of unity and cultural pride. The symbolism associated with Kimpa Vita is rich and enduring. In the eyes of her followers, she represents the strength to challenge the status quo and the wisdom to embrace a new spiritual vision. Her life and teachings continue to inspire those who seek to balance tradition with innovation.

The impact of Kimpa Vita on Kongo society was profound, her teachings uniting spiritual beliefs across the kingdom. She called for a return to the core values of community and cooperation, challenging the fragmentation that had weakened the kingdom. Her vision of a unified spiritual practice inspired rituals and ceremonies that blended African traditions with Christian elements, creating a unique religious identity that resonated with her people. These practices became a source of strength and identity, reinforcing a sense of belonging and purpose. Kimpa Vita's influence extended to the rituals and practices that continue to shape Kongo spirituality. Her teachings encouraged the incorporation of African symbols and traditions into Christian worship, offering a sense of continuity and cultural pride. This integration fostered a deeper connection to the past, allowing her followers to embrace their heritage while adapting to new spiritual landscapes. Through these practices, Kimpa Vita's legacy lives on, her vision of unity and spiritual renewal continuing to inspire and guide.

In the myths and stories that surround Kimpa Vita, her divine mission is a central theme. One such tale speaks of her journey, guided by visions of St. Anthony, to restore the kingdom of Kongo to its rightful place of prominence. Her mission was not just a political endeavor but a spiritual calling, one that sought to heal the divisions within her community. Myths depict Kimpa Vita as a bridge between the divine and mortal worlds, her role as a guide and protector of the Kongo people firmly embedded in the cultural consciousness. These stories serve as a testament to her enduring influence, highlighting her role as a spiritual and cultural leader. Through these narratives, Kimpa Vita's impact is felt, her teachings continuing to inspire those who seek to honor their heritage and embrace a vision of unity and renewal. In this way, Kimpa Vita's legacy endures, a powerful reminder of the strength and resilience that lies within the African spirit.

MBOKOMU: THE MOTHER EARTH AND FERTILITY DEITY

In the lush heartlands of Central Africa, where the earth teems with life, and the air is rich with the scent of blooming flora, the presence of Mbokomu is felt in every leaf and every grain of soil. She is revered as the Mother Earth, a divine embodiment of fertility and abundance, nurturing the land and its people. Mbokomu's influence is vast, reaching into the roots of the crops that sustain life and extending to the hearts of those who call upon her for guidance and protection. As a fertility deity, her blessings ensure the prosperity of the fields, the richness of the harvest, and the continuation of life. Her nurturing spirit is a source of comfort, a reminder of the earth's capacity to provide and sustain. In times of need, it is to Mbokomu that communities turn, seeking her favor to bring rain to parched lands or to bless the soil with the promise of plenty.

The myths surrounding Mbokomu paint her as a powerful and benevolent force. One such story tells of the time when the earth was barren and devoid of life. Mbokomu, seeing the desolation, bestowed her gifts upon the land, breathing life into the seeds buried deep within the soil. The legend of Mbokomu and the birth of crops speaks to her role as the bringer of abundance, a force that revitalizes and renews. In this tale, she is depicted as moving through the fields, her touch awakening dormant seeds and transforming them into thriving plants. Her influence extends beyond agriculture, touching the lives of women and children, whom she guides and protects. Myths recount her aid in childbirth, where her gentle presence ensures the safe delivery of new life, and her wisdom guides mothers in nurturing their children. Through these stories, Mbokomu's role as a caretaker and life-giver is celebrated, her spirit woven into the fabric of everyday life.

In the art and iconography of Central Africa, Mbokomu is represented through symbols that speak to her connection with the earth and its bounty. The earth itself is a powerful symbol of her domain, embodying the fertile soil that sustains life and the cycle of growth and renewal. Plants and fertility symbols, such as seeds and budding flowers, are common motifs in her depictions, representing the potential for life and the promise of new beginnings. These symbols are not just artistic expressions; they are sacred reminders of Mbokomu's presence and her role as the guardian of fertility. In various artistic traditions, Mbokomu may be portrayed with elements that highlight her nurturing qualities, such as holding a child or being surrounded by crops. These portrayals capture her essence as a nurturing mother, a deity whose love and care nourish both the earth and its inhabitants.

The rituals and practices that honor Mbokomu are vibrant celebrations of life and abundance. Offerings of seeds and earth are central to these rituals, symbolic acts that acknowledge her role in the cycle of growth and renewal. These tributes are made at sacred sites, such as fields and gardens, where her presence is believed to be strongest. Through these rituals, communities express gratitude for the blessings they've received and seek her continued favor for future prosperity. Annual festivals celebrate Mbokomu's influence, bringing together people in joyful homage to Mother Earth. During these celebrations, music and dance play a crucial role, with participants moving in harmony with the rhythms of the earth. These festivals are not just religious observances; they are communal gatherings that reinforce the bonds between individuals and their connection to the land. Through these practices, the relationship between humans and Mbokomu is honored and renewed, ensuring that the cycle of life continues to thrive.

As we conclude our exploration of the Central African pantheon, we've delved into the rich tapestry of deities and spiritual figures that shape the beliefs and practices of these communities. From the sky to the earth, each deity holds a unique place in the spiritual landscape, reflecting the diverse ways in which people connect with the divine. As we move forward, we'll turn our attention to the South African pantheon, where new stories and traditions await.

UNKULUNKULU   MODJADJI   THIXO

CHAPTER 4: SOUTHERN AFRICAN PANTHEON

I magine a land where the horizon stretches wide, where the mountains stand tall against the sky, and where every dawn brings the promise of a new day. In the spiritual heart of the Xhosa people, this land is not just a physical space but a canvas painted by the hands of Qamata, the Supreme Creator. Qamata's presence is woven into the very fabric of existence, the unseen force that shapes the world. As the originator of life, Qamata holds a revered place in Xhosa cosmology, a god whose story begins at the dawn of time. It is said that before the world took shape, there was only chaos and void. Qamata, with a vision of harmony and life, reached into this nothingness, crafting the heavens and the earth with divine intent. The mountains, the rivers, the skies—all were born from his will. His creation extends to the first humans, molded with care and purpose, each a testament to his mastery over life.

Qamata's role as the supreme creator doesn't end with the act of creation; it extends to the delegation of tasks to other deities and spirits. These entities, guided by Qamata, act as stewards of the world, each responsible for a specific aspect of life. They serve as intermediaries between the divine and the earthly, ensuring that the balance of nature and humanity is maintained. This delegation reflects Qamata's wisdom, an understanding that harmony arises from collaboration and shared responsibility. The spirits, often appearing in dreams or visions, communicate the divine will, offering guidance and insight to those who seek it. Through these interactions, Qamata maintains a relationship with humanity, a connection that informs and influences the lives of the Xhosa people.

In the art and cultural practices of the Xhosa, Qamata's attributes are celebrated and revered. Omnipotence and wisdom are the hallmarks of his character, qualities that inspire both awe and devotion. The sun, a powerful symbol of Qamata, represents the cycle of life, a reminder of the divine light that sustains all existence. In artistic depictions, the color white is often used to signify Qamata's purity and transcendence, a hue that embodies the divine presence in rituals and ceremonies. Temples and sacred spaces dedicated to Qamata serve as focal points for worship, places where the physical and spiritual worlds converge, allowing the faithful to connect with the divine. These spaces are adorned with symbols and motifs that honor Qamata's legacy, each element a reflection of his enduring influence.

The myths that surround Qamata are rich with meaning and significance, offering insight into his role as a guiding force in Xhosa belief. One such myth tells of the creation of the mountains, where Qamata, in his desire to protect the land, raised the earth to form towering peaks. These mountains stood as guardians, shielding the people from harm and providing a foundation for life. This story underscores Qamata's protective nature and his commitment to the well-being of his creation. Other tales speak of Qamata's guidance to the Xhosa people, where his wisdom and foresight illuminate the path to prosperity and peace. His interventions in significant historical events highlight his active role in shaping the destiny of his followers, ensuring that they remain aligned with the divine plan.

In Xhosa religious practices, the veneration of Qamata is a vibrant expression of faith and gratitude. Ceremonies and offerings dedicated to Qamata are central to these practices, acts of devotion that seek his blessing and favor. Shamans and priests play a crucial role in facilitating this connection, their chants and prayers reaching out to Qamata, inviting his presence and guidance. These spiritual leaders are entrusted with the sacred duty of maintaining the bond between the people and the divine. Annual festivals celebrate Qamata's contributions, gatherings that bring the community together in joyful homage. These events are marked by music, dance, and the sharing of stories, creating an atmosphere of unity and reverence. Through these practices, the relationship between the Xhosa and Qamata is honored and renewed, a testament to the enduring power of faith and tradition.

Reflection Section: Your Connection to Qamata

Reflect on the stories and attributes of Qamata. Consider how these elements resonate with your own beliefs and experiences. How do they connect you to your roots and cultural heritage? Use this space to jot down your thoughts and insights, exploring the ways in which these stories enrich your understanding of the world and your place within it.

UNKULUNKULU: THE GREAT ANCESTOR OF THE ZULU

Imagine the first moments of creation through the eyes of the Zulu people. Emerging from the reeds of the primordial waters, Unkulunkulu, the Great Ancestor, stepped forth to shape the world. His emergence marked the dawn of humanity, as he took the raw elements of earth and molded them with care. The reeds, which cradled Unkulunkulu, hold a sacred place in Zulu mythology, symbolizing the source of life and the connection between the divine and the terrestrial. As the progenitor of all humans, Unkulunkulu's hands crafted the first beings, instilling them with the breath of life and the essence of his spirit. This act of creation was not just about the physical formation of humans; it represented the planting of a seed, one that would grow into the rich tapestry of the Zulu nation.

Unkulunkulu embodies strength and fertility, qualities that resonate deeply within Zulu culture. His image is one of power and vitality, a figure who commands respect and reverence. In Zulu art and cultural expressions, Unkulunkulu is often represented through symbols that highlight these attributes. The use of natural motifs, such as reeds and water, serves as a reminder of his role as the life-giver and sustainer. Reeds, in particular, are a potent symbol, reflecting the resilience and adaptability of the Zulu people. They represent the ability to bend without breaking, to thrive in diverse environments. Through these symbols, Unkulunkulu's presence is felt, his influence woven into the cultural fabric of Zulu life.

The stories of Unkulunkulu are rich with lessons and insights, providing guidance and wisdom to those who seek it. One such myth recounts the creation of the Zulu nation, a tale that speaks to the unity and strength of the people. In this story, Unkulunkulu is portrayed as a wise leader, guiding his followers with compassion and understanding. His teachings emphasize the importance of community and cooperation, values that are central to Zulu identity. Another tale highlights Unkulunkulu's interactions with other deities and spirits, where his wisdom and foresight play a pivotal role in maintaining harmony and balance. These stories are more than just narratives; they are a source of inspiration and reflection, offering a window into the values and beliefs that define the Zulu people.

In Zulu religious practices, the veneration of Unkulunkulu is a deeply rooted tradition, one that honors his role as the Great Ancestor. Rituals involving offerings of food and drink are a central aspect of these practices, acts of devotion that seek to honor Unkulunkulu's contributions to life and creation. These offerings are made with care and intention, each item chosen for its symbolic significance. The role of sangomas, or traditional healers, is crucial in these rituals, as they act as intermediaries between the earthly and the divine. Their chants and incantations reach out to Unkulunkulu, inviting his presence and blessing. Annual festivals and ceremonies celebrate Unkulunkulu's legacy, bringing together communities in joyful homage. These events are marked by music, dance, and storytelling, creating an atmosphere of unity and reverence. Through these practices, the relationship between the Zulu people and Unkulunkulu is strengthened, ensuring that his legacy continues to inspire and guide future generations.

MODJADJI: THE RAIN QUEEN OF THE LOVEDU

In the lush landscapes of the BaLobedu people, where each rain drop is a blessing and the land thrives under its nourishing embrace, the figure of Modjadji, the Rain Queen, stands as a central force. Her presence is felt in the rhythmic patter of rain on leaves, a reminder of the life-giving power she wields. Known for her ability to control the weather and summon rain, Modjadji's influence is profound, touching every aspect of BaLobedu agriculture and daily existence. In a region where the land's fertility depends on the rains, her role as a rainmaker is not just a duty but a sacred trust. Her connection to the skies ensures that the fields are watered, the rivers run deep, and the people are fed. The rain she brings is more than just water; it is the promise of life and prosperity, a gift that sustains communities and nurtures the bonds between people and the earth.

Modjadji's legacy is one of power tempered by benevolence. She is revered not only for her extraordinary abilities but also for her wisdom and compassion. In BaLobedu art and cultural practices, Modjadji is often depicted through symbols of rain and water, reflecting her central role in the cycle of life. The imagery of clouds and rainstorms are common motifs, capturing the dynamic and nurturing aspects of her nature. These symbols serve as reminders of her enduring presence, her spirit woven into the cultural fabric of the BaLobedu people. Her legacy extends beyond her lifetime, with each

Rain Queen inheriting the mantle of her predecessor, ensuring that the traditions and responsibilities are passed down through generations. This continuity is a testament to the enduring power of her role, one that commands respect and admiration across the region. Modjadji's ability to bring rain is seen as both a miracle and a necessity, a divine intervention that maintains the delicate balance of nature.

The myths surrounding Modjadji are rich and varied, each telling a story of her divine lineage and miraculous abilities. One such tale speaks of her origins, tracing her ancestry to a powerful line of rainmakers who possessed the knowledge of the skies. According to legend, Modjadji was chosen by the spirits to carry on this legacy, her birth marked by signs and omens that foretold her future greatness. Another story recounts a time of drought, when the land was parched and the people desperate for relief. Modjadji, with her connection to the divine, called upon the spirits, summoning the rains that quenched the earth's thirst and restored life to the land. Her interactions with other deities and spirits highlight her role as a mediator, a bridge between the earthly and the divine realms. Through these stories, Modjadji's importance is underscored, her influence shaping the destinies of those who honor her.

The veneration of Modjadji is a vibrant expression of faith and gratitude, reflected in the rituals and practices that honor her contributions. Ceremonies dedicated to Modjadji are central to BaLobedu religious life, acts of devotion that seek her blessing and favor. Offerings of water, flowers, and symbolic items are made with reverence, each chosen for its significance in connecting with the Rain Queen. The royal family plays a pivotal role in these practices, ensuring that the rituals are carried out with the respect and dignity they deserve. Their involvement underscores the deep connection between the Rain Queen and the community, a bond that is both spiritual and cultural. Annual festivals celebrating Modjadji's contributions are a time of joy and renewal, gatherings that bring the community together in shared homage. These events are marked by music, dance, and storytelling, creating an atmosphere of celebration and unity. Through these practices, the relationship between the BaLobedu people and Modjadji is honored and maintained, ensuring that her legacy continues to inspire and sustain future generations.

THIXO: THE SKY GOD AND HIS INFLUENCE

High above the bustling world of Southern Africa, where the land meets the heavens, resides Thixo, the revered sky god. His domain is vast, stretching across the boundless sky where he orchestrates the cosmic dance of the sun, moon, and stars. As the deity of the sky, Thixo wields control over these celestial bodies, guiding their movements with divine precision. The sun rises and sets at his command, bringing light and warmth to the earth. The moon, with its gentle glow, follows its path under Thixo's watchful eye, while the stars twinkle in the night sky, forming constellations that tell stories of old. This celestial ballet is not just a display of beauty; it is a testament to Thixo's power and omnipresence, a reminder of the divine order that governs the universe.

Thixo's influence extends beyond the heavens, reaching into the daily lives of those who depend on the land for sustenance. His control over weather patterns directly impacts agriculture, determining the cycles of planting and harvest. When the rains fall, nourishing the soil, it is Thixo's blessing that ensures the crops grow strong and bountiful. In the dry season, it is his restraint that teaches patience and resilience. The rhythms of nature, the ebb and flow of life's cycles, are all under Thixo's domain. Through his guidance, the earth remains fertile, and the people prosper, finding balance in the natural world. Thixo's role as a guardian of the seasons is crucial, as he oversees the transitions that mark the passage of time.

In the rich tapestry of Southern African art and culture, Thixo's attributes are celebrated and revered. Representations of power and omnipresence are common motifs, capturing the essence of a deity whose reach is infinite. Celestial symbols, such as suns, moons, and stars, are woven into art and cultural expressions, reflecting Thixo's role as the master of the skies. These symbols are not mere decorations; they are reminders of the divine connection that binds the earthly to the celestial. Through these artistic expressions, Thixo's presence is felt, his influence permeating the cultural landscape. The imagery of celestial bodies serves as a reminder of the divine order, a reflection of the interconnectedness of all things.

The myths that surround Thixo are rich with meaning and significance, offering insight into his role as a guiding force. One such myth tells of Thixo's creation of the cosmos, where he shaped the universe from chaos, bringing order and harmony to the celestial realm. This story speaks to his power as a creator, a force of nature that commands respect and reverence. Another tale recounts Thixo's role in guiding the seasons and agricultural cycles, ensuring that the earth remains fertile and life continues to thrive. These are not just narratives; they're lessons in balance and harmony, reflecting the values that underpin Southern African culture. Thixo's interactions with other deities and spirits highlight his role as a mediator, a bridge between the earthly and divine realms.

The veneration of Thixo is a vibrant expression of faith and gratitude, reflected in the rituals and practices that honor his contributions. Offerings of food and drink are central to these practices, acts of devotion that seek to honor Thixo's role in sustaining life. Traditional healers play a crucial role in these rituals, acting as intermediaries between the earthly and the divine. Their chants and prayers reach out to Thixo, inviting his presence and blessing. Annual festivals and ceremonies celebrate Thixo's legacy, bringing communities together in joyful homage. These events are marked by music, dance, and storytelling, creating an atmosphere of unity and reverence. Through these practices, the relationship between the people and Thixo is honored and maintained, ensuring that his legacy continues to inspire and guide future generations.

In the vast expanse of the skies of Southern Africa, Thixo's presence is a constant; a reminder of the divine forces that shape our world. His influence touches every aspect of life, from the celestial to the earthly, guiding us with wisdom and grace. As we conclude our exploration of the Southern African pantheon, we find ourselves connected to the stories and traditions that define these cultures. Through Thixo, we are reminded of the power of the divine, a force that transcends time and space, guiding us on our journey through life.

CREATION MYTHS

YORUBA   KONGO   ZULU

CHAPTER 5: COMPARATIVE MYTHOLOGICAL ANALYSIS: CREATION MYTHS

C reation myths offer a window into the soul of a culture, revealing not just how a people understand the origins of the world, but also how they see their place within it. Through these narratives, we find explanations not only for the physical formation of the earth but also for the invisible threads that bind humanity, Nature, and the divine. This chapter will explore three African creation myths: those of the Yoruba, Kongo, and Zulu peoples. Each of these myths tells a story of beginnings, filled with symbolism, cultural values, and the unique relationships between humans and the divine.

The Yoruba creation myth introduces us to Olodumare, the supreme creator, and his decision to delegate the task of creation to the Orishas. One may classify Orishas as deities, but that would understate their existence and importance. To be succinct, they are forces of Nature and manifest from a deity's will, order, or desire to accomplish a goal. They can rise from Nature, or an honored ancestor may transform into such an entity. Essentially, Orishas are vital in influencing events that directly impact humanity and its progress in the world.

Olodumare entrusts Obatala, the Orisha of wisdom and purity, with shaping the earth using a snail shell, a rooster, and a palm nut. Through these items, land is formed, and the first tree sprouts, illustrating the Yoruba belief in a collective effort. When Obatala, intoxicated by palm wine, creates humanity, he introduces imperfections, which the Yoruba see as a reflection of life's diversity and the beauty of uniqueness.

In the Kongo creation myth, Nzambi a Mpungu, the supreme god, shapes the earth and brings forth water—a life-giving force symbolizing interconnectedness. Nzambi a Mpungu establishes natural laws and delegates roles to spiritual beings, maintaining harmony within creation. He actively participates in ensuring that every part of the world functions as intended, reflecting the cultural appreciation for unity and balance.

The Zulu creation story centers on Unkulunkulu, the great ancestor who emerges from the reeds, symbolizing the beginning of life. Unkulunkulu crafts humans and animals, breathing life into the earth and introducing social norms and community values. The Zulu myth emphasizes harmony—between people, Nature, and within the self—forming the foundation of Zulu culture.

Together, these three creation myths offer a rich tapestry of African cosmology, each reflecting the values and worldview of the culture from which it originates. The Yoruba myth emphasizes the power of collaboration and the acceptance of imperfection. The Kongo narrative underscores the importance of natural balance and the interconnectedness of all things. The Zulu story celebrates the nurturing role of the creator and the foundational values of community and cooperation. Through these myths, we see a common thread—a deep reverence for life, a recognition of the interconnectedness of all beings, and an understanding that creation is an ongoing, collective journey.

As we delve into these stories, we are invited to see the world through the eyes of these cultures, to appreciate the wisdom embedded in their narratives, and to reflect on our own relationship with the world around us. Creation, after all, is not a singular event confined to the past; it is a continuous process, one that we are all a part of, shaping and reshaping the world with every action, every decision, and every breath.

YORUBA CREATION MYTH: OLUDUMARE AND OBATALA

Have you ever stood on the edge of a riverbank, watching the current carry leaves downstream, and wondered about the origins of the world? In Yoruba mythology, the creation story begins not with a bang or a flood but with a quiet moment of delegation.

At the heart of this myth lies Olodumare, the supreme creator, who envisioned a world vibrant with life and complexity. But Olodumare, recognizing the magnitude of the task, didn't set out to create the world alone. Instead, he entrusted the work to the Orishas, those powerful deities who would bring his vision to life, each contributing their unique gifts to the fabric of creation.

Olodumare's delegation of tasks begins with Obatala, the Orisha of wisdom and purity. He descends to the formless earth with three humble items: a snail shell filled with sand, a rooster, and a palm nut. These items, seemingly mundane, hold the key to shaping the world. Obatala spreads the sand from the snail shell, forming the earth's surface, while the rooster scratches and scatters it, creating mountains and valleys. The palm nut, planted with care, becomes the first tree, a symbol of life and growth. In this act, Obatala sets the stage for the world's transformation, a transformation that mirrors the gentle unfolding of a new day.

With the earth taking shape, Obatala turns his attention to the creation of humanity. He molds figures from clay, crafting each one with precision and care. The clay, malleable and full of potential, represents the possibilities within every human being. Yet, as the story unfolds, Obatala is overcome by the temptations of palm wine, leading to a moment of intoxication. In his altered state, some of the figures he creates are imperfect, a reflection of the diversity and uniqueness found within humanity. This moment of imperfection is not a flaw but a testament to the richness of life, where beauty and diversity coexist.

As Obatala rests, Oduduwa steps in to complete the creation. Known as the founder of the Yoruba people, Oduduwa's role is crucial. He ensures that the world is structured correctly, laying the foundation for societies to flourish. His intervention highlights the theme of cooperation and unity among the Orishas. Meanwhile, Orunmila, the deity of wisdom and divination, offers guidance and insight, ensuring that the creation aligns with the divine plan. Orunmila's presence is a reminder of the importance of wisdom and foresight in shaping the world.

Eshu, the trickster and messenger, plays a vital role in maintaining balance and communication between heaven and earth. His presence ensures that messages and offerings flow smoothly between the divine and the mortal realms. Eshu's ability to navigate both worlds highlights the interconnectedness of all things, a theme that resonates throughout the Yoruba creation myth. His role as a mediator ensures that harmony is maintained, allowing the divine plan to unfold without disruption.

The symbolic elements within the Yoruba creation story are rich with meaning and insight. The snail shell and sand represent the earth's formation, symbolizing stability and foundation. The act of spreading sand is akin to spreading life across the world, each grain a potential for growth. The palm nut, a symbol of life and growth, speaks to the interconnectedness of all living things, a reminder of the cycles of birth, death, and rebirth. Using clay to create humans underscores the malleability and potential inherent in humanity, a reflection of our ability to shape our destinies.

Compared to other creation myths, the Yoruba narrative stands out for its emphasis on divine delegation and cooperation among deities. Unlike myths where a single god governs the process, the Yoruba story highlights the importance of collaboration, with each Orisha contributing their unique strengths. This theme of cooperation is mirrored in the values of the Yoruba people, where community and harmony are central to achieving common goals. The natural elements of earth, water, and plants play a crucial role in the creation, reflecting the deep connection between the divine and the natural world.

While some creation myths focus on a supreme deity's omnipotence, the Yoruba story presents a more nuanced portrayal. Olodumare's choice to delegate tasks reflects a recognition of the complexity and interconnectedness of life. This approach emphasizes the importance of balance and harmony, themes echoed in the Orishas' roles. Through their actions, the world is not just created but nurtured and sustained, ensuring that life continues to thrive.

As you reflect on the Yoruba creation myth, consider how these themes of cooperation, balance, and growth resonate with your own experiences. The story offers a rich tapestry of insights and wisdom, inviting us to explore the depths of our own potential and the connections that bind us to the world. The symbols and narratives within this myth continue to inspire, reminding us of the power and beauty inherent in creation.

THE KONGO CREATION MYTH: NZAMBI A MPUNGU AND THE BIRTH OF THE WORLD

In the heart of Kongo spirituality, the vastness of the universe begins with Nzambi a Mpungu, the eternal Sky Father, who crafted the world in a dance of creation that was as deliberate as it was magnificent. Picture the scene: a formless void, silent and waiting. Nzambi a Mpungu, with his infinite wisdom, reaches out and parts the chaos, separating the earth from the sky. This act of separation is not just an act of creation; it is a declaration of order, a foundation upon which life can flourish. With the earth beneath and the sky above, Nzambi a Mpungu sets the stage for a world teeming with life and potential.

From the newly formed earth arise the first waters, flowing with the promise of sustenance and life. Nzambi a Mpungu's creation of water is more than just a physical act; it is a gift, a vital force that nurtures and sustains all living things. As rivers carve their paths through the land, they convey the essence of life, a reminder of the interconnectedness of all things. The next step in Nzambi a Mpungu's grand design is the creation of the first humans and animals. With care and intention, he molds them from the earth, breathing life into their forms. Each creature, from the smallest insect to the most majestic beast, is crafted with purpose, a testament to his boundless creativity.

But Nzambi a Mpungu's work does not end with the physical world. He establishes natural laws and order, embedding them into the fabric of creation. These laws govern the cycles of life and death, nature's rhythms that ensure balance and harmony. They are the unseen forces that guide the world, a reflection of his wisdom and foresight. Beyond the tangible, Nzambi a Mpungu also creates spiritual beings, assigning them roles that maintain the delicate equilibrium of the cosmos. These beings, each with their own domain and responsibilities, act as guardians and guides, ensuring that the world functions as intended.

Nzambi a Mpungu's attributes and actions in this creation narrative speak to his omnipotence and wisdom. He is not a distant god but an active participant in the world he has created. His decisions are deliberate, each reflecting a deep understanding of the complexities of life. In his wisdom, Nzambi a Mpungu delegates tasks to lesser spirits and deities, recognizing that the world is too vast for one being to manage alone. This delegation is not a sign of weakness but of strength, an acknowledgment of the power that lies in collaboration and unity. Through this network of spiritual beings, Nzambi a Mpungu ensures that the world remains in harmony, each element playing its part in the grand symphony of creation.

The symbolic elements in the Kongo creation story are rich with meaning, each offering insight into the values and beliefs of the Kongo people. The separation of earth and sky is a powerful symbol of order and structure, a reminder that even amid chaos, there is potential for harmony. This act of separation establishes a framework for life, creating distinct realms that interact and coexist. The creation of water as a source of life and sustenance highlights its central role in the cycle of life, a vital force that connects all living things. Water is both a physical necessity and a spiritual symbol, representing the fluidity and adaptability required to thrive in a changing world.

The establishment of natural laws by Nzambi a Mpungu represents harmony and balance, principles central to the Kongo worldview. These laws govern the interactions between both physical and spiritual beings, ensuring that the world operates in a state of equilibrium. They reflect the understanding that balance is not static but dynamic, a continuous process of adjustment and adaptation. The spiritual beings created by Nzambi a Mpungu are not just caretakers but active participants in this process, their roles integral to maintaining harmony.

When comparing the Kongo creation myth to other creation stories, both African and global, certain themes stand out. The theme of divine creation and the establishment of natural order is a common thread, seen in myths from various cultures. However, the Kongo story's emphasis on the delegation of tasks and the collaboration between Nzambi a Mpungu and the spiritual beings is unique, highlighting the importance of cooperation in achieving balance. This approach contrasts with myths where a single deity assumes complete control, offering a more nuanced view of divine governance.

The portrayal of spiritual beings in the Kongo myth differs from other creation narratives, where these entities often serve as mere extensions of the supreme deity's will. In the Kongo story, these beings have distinct roles and responsibilities, acting with a degree of autonomy that reflects the complexity of the world they inhabit. This portrayal emphasizes the interconnectedness of all things, a theme that resonates with the Kongo belief in the unity of the physical and spiritual realms. Through these comparisons, the Kongo creation myth offers a rich tapestry of insights, inviting us to explore the depths of its wisdom and the beauty of its narrative.

THE ZULU CREATION STORY: UNKULUNKULU AND THE ORIGINS OF HUMANITY

Imagine a time when the world was just beginning to find its form, the earth was young, and the air was filled with the promise of new life. From this primordial landscape emerged Unkulunkulu, the great ancestor of the Zulu people, stepping forth from the reeds that cradled him. These humble yet significant reeds are more than mere plants; they symbolize the source of life and the beginning of everything. As Unkulunkulu emerged, he brought the seeds of creation, ready to shape the world with the wisdom and care of a nurturing parent.

Unkulunkulu's first act as the creator was to breathe life into the earth, molding the first humans and animals with his own hands. Each creature, crafted with intention, reflected his vision for a world teeming with life and diversity. The humans, formed from the earth itself, were given the gift of consciousness and the ability to shape their own destinies. Animals, each unique in form and function, filled the land with movement and sound, contributing to the vibrant tapestry of existence. Through Unkulunkulu's touch, the world came alive, a symphony of sounds and sights that echoed the divine harmony of creation.

Beyond the physical creation of beings, Unkulunkulu played a pivotal role in establishing the social and cultural norms that would guide humanity. As the great ancestor and progenitor, he was more than just a creator; he was a teacher, imparting the skills and knowledge needed to thrive in the world he had crafted. He introduced the concepts of community and cooperation, laying the foundation for societies to flourish. Unkulunkulu's teachings emphasized the importance of harmony and respect, values that would become the bedrock of Zulu culture. His guidance was a beacon, illuminating the path to a life of balance and fulfillment.

One of Unkulunkulu's most significant contributions was the introduction of tools, fire, and agriculture to humanity. These gifts were more than just practical innovations; they were symbols of human progress and civilization. Tools allowed people to shape their environment, build and create, and transform the landscape to suit their needs. Fire, a source of warmth and protection, also represented the spark of creativity and the potential for transformation. Agriculture, the cultivation of the earth, was a testament to humanity's ability to harness the natural world for sustenance and growth. Through these gifts, Unkulunkulu empowered humanity to take control of their destiny and to build societies that reflected the divine order of creation.

The symbolic elements within the Zulu creation story are rich with meaning, each offering insights into the values and beliefs that define the Zulu people. The reeds from which Unkulunkulu emerged are a potent symbol of life and fertility, a reminder of the interconnectedness of all living things. They represent the potential for growth and renewal, a cycle that mirrors the rhythms of nature. The creation of tools and fire symbolizes the progress and evolution of humanity and the ability to innovate and adapt in the face of challenges. Agriculture, as a representation of sustenance and growth, underscores the importance of nurturing and cultivating the earth, reflecting the symbiotic relationship between humans and their environment.

When comparing the Zulu creation myth to other creation stories, both African and global, certain narratives coalesce. The theme of divine emergence and the nurturing of humanity is a common thread, reflecting the idea that creation is not just an act of formation but a process of care and guidance. Unlike myths where the divine remains distant, the Zulu narrative emphasizes the active role of a progenitor deity in teaching and guiding humanity. Unkulunkulu's involvement in establishing societal structures and cultural norms sets the Zulu story apart, highlighting the importance of community and cooperation in achieving harmony.

The portrayal of Unkulunkulu as both creator and teacher offers a unique perspective on the relationship between the divine and humanity. This dual role reflects the understanding that creation is an ongoing process, one that requires continuous engagement and evolution. Through Unkulunkulu's actions, the Zulu people are reminded of their connection to the divine, a bond that informs their identity and purpose. These themes resonate with the broader human experience, offering a lens through which we can explore our own origins and aspirations.

As we reflect on the Zulu creation story, we're drawn into a narrative that speaks to the heart of what it means to be human. Through the actions and teachings of Unkulunkulu, we find a mirror that reflects our own potential and our capacity for growth and transformation. The symbols and stories within this myth invite us to consider the ways in which we can nurture and cultivate our own lives, embrace the gifts of creation, and use them to build a world of harmony and balance. In doing so, we honor the legacy of Unkulunkulu, the great ancestor whose vision continues to inspire and guide us.

CHAPTER 6: COMPARATIVE MYTHOLOGICAL ANALYSIS: TRICKSTER ARCHETYPES

Trickster archetypes are a fascinating and integral part of mythology, symbolizing disruption, transformation, and the complexities of human nature. These figures, who often blur the lines between good and evil, embody the unpredictable forces that shape both the physical and spiritual realms. This chapter will explore four prominent African trickster archetypes: Eshu of the Yoruba, Anansi of the Ashanti, Legba of the Fon, and Hare of Southern African folklore. Each trickster is unique, yet they share common traits that reveal profound insights into human behavior and cultural values.

In Yoruba mythology, Eshu is the trickster of the crossroads, a place of choices and change. Eshu is both a disruptor and a mediator, embodying duality—chaos and order, troublemaker and messenger. His antics often reveal profound truths about perspective and understanding. For example, in the tale of the divided village, Eshu wears a hat that is red on one side and black on the other, stirring conflict among the villagers. Eshu is a figure who challenges and instructs, ensuring that messages between gods and humans are delivered, while also testing the integrity of those he encounters.

Anansi, the spider from Ashanti folklore, is a master of cunning and storytelling. His tales explore themes of wit and strategy, often highlighting the value of cleverness over brute strength. In the story of Anansi and the sky god Nyame, Anansi uses his ingenuity to complete impossible tasks, ultimately gaining the right to tell stories. His actions show that intelligence and resourcefulness can overcome seemingly insurmountable obstacles. However, Anansi's character is complex; his greed and mischief often lead to unintended consequences. Anansi's stories serve as both entertainment and moral instruction, revealing the dual nature of wisdom—it is powerful, but only when shared.

Legba, the trickster from Fon mythology, stands as the gatekeeper of the crossroads, a figure who facilitates communication between the divine and human worlds. Legba's role is one of balance—he can open paths or create obstacles, depending on the lessons that need to be taught. Legba's influence is not merely disruptive; it is also deeply instructive, emphasizing the importance of humility and respect in human relationships.

Hare, a trickster from Southern African folklore, is known for his quick thinking and unmatched cleverness. Hare's tales are filled with humor and wit, often demonstrating the triumph of intelligence over brute strength. One story concerning a powerful lion illustrates the importance of using wit to overcome adversity. However, Hare's antics are not always without consequences, as his tricks sometimes lead to trouble, reminding listeners of the delicate balance between cleverness and responsibility.

These four tricksters—Eshu, Anansi, Legba, and Hare—represent the unpredictable elements of life, challenging the established order while providing valuable lessons about human nature. Through their stories, we gain insight into the importance of adaptability, perspective, and humility. The trickster archetype embodies the tension between chaos and order, pushing us to question our assumptions and encouraging growth through reflection and change.

As we explore the tales of these tricksters, we are invited to see beyond their mischief and recognize the wisdom they impart. They remind us that life is not always straightforward; it is full of crossroads, challenges, and opportunities for transformation. By embracing the lessons of these archetypal figures, we can learn to navigate the complexities of our own lives with greater understanding, creativity, and resilience.

ESHU: THE TRICKSTER AND THE STOLEN YAM

You've probably heard the saying that life is what happens at the crossroads. It's a place of choices and change, where paths meet and destinies unfold. In Yoruba mythology, the crossroads belong to Eshu, the trickster and divine messenger—the one who thrives in the in-between spaces. Eshu is a master of duality, embodying both chaos and order, a figure who challenges the status quo while maintaining the delicate balance of the universe. He is not just a troublemaker; he's a mediator, a bridge between the gods and humans, ensuring that messages travel smoothly across realms. This dual nature makes him such a fascinating character who can both cause and resolve conflicts with a flick of his wrist.

Eshu's ability to stir the pot is legendary, yet it's not chaos for chaos's sake. His actions often carry deeper meanings, teaching lessons that resonate far beyond the immediate. Take, for instance, the story of Eshu and the divided village. In this tale, Eshu wears a hat that's red on one side and black on the other. As he strolls down the village path, he creates a rift among the villagers, each group convinced they're right about the hat's color. It's a simple trick, yet it uncovers a profound truth: perspective shapes reality. By manipulating this, Eshu shows that understanding and empathy are crucial to resolving conflicts, turning division into unity.

Another tale of Eshu's cunning involves a king who prided himself on his integrity. Eshu, ever the tester of character, decides to put this to the test by disguising himself as a beggar. Unaware of Eshu's true identity, the king dismisses the beggar harshly. Later, when Eshu reveals himself, the king must face the harsh truth of his actions. This story serves as a reminder that true integrity isn't just about how we present ourselves; it's about how we treat others, regardless of their status. Through his trickery, Eshu imparts wisdom, pushing us to reflect on our moral compass and the values we hold dear.

In the myth of Eshu and the stolen yam, Eshu's cleverness uncovers a thief in the most unexpected way. A series of thefts plagued the village, and no one could determine who was responsible. Eshu, with his knack for turning the ordinary into the extraordinary, sprinkled yam flour on the path leading from the village. As the thief walked, the flour stuck to his feet, leaving a trail that led straight to his door. It's a classic trickster tale, one that highlights Eshu's role as a bringer of justice, using wit and ingenuity to restore balance.

Eshu's symbolism is as rich and layered as the stories themselves. The crossroads, a powerful symbol in his mythology, represents choice and destiny. It's where paths intersect, and decisions must be made, embodying the complexity of life's journey. In Yoruba art, Eshu is often depicted with the colors red and black, which symbolize his dual nature—passion and mystery, chaos and order. These colors adorn his altars and offerings, a testament to his multifaceted character. In iconography, Eshu might be shown with a mischievous smile, a visual reminder of his playful yet profound influence on the world.

In Yoruba religious practices, Eshu holds a revered place, a deity whose presence is invoked in daily life. His role in Ifa divination is crucial, as he opens the channels of communication between the earthly and the divine. Those in need call upon Eshu to bless their endeavors, ensuring clarity and truth in the insights they seek. Rituals dedicated to Eshu often involve offerings like kola nuts or palm oil, each chosen for its symbolic significance. These acts of devotion acknowledge Eshu's power and seek his favor, maintaining a dynamic relationship between the people and the divine. Eshu's significance extends to festivals and celebrations, where his stories are told, and his influence is celebrated through music, dance, and communal gatherings.

ANANSI: THE SPIDER TRICKSTER OF THE ASHANTI

Anansi, the spider, is a figure who dances deftly between the roles of hero and deceiver, his web of tales stretching across the rich landscape of Ashanti (Asante) folklore. Known for his cleverness and unmatched resourcefulness, Anansi is the quintessential trickster, a master of cunning who often finds himself at the center of stories that challenge the boundaries of right and wrong. His tales are more than mere entertainment; they serve as vessels of cultural wisdom, carrying lessons of strategy, wit, and the complexities of human nature. Anansi embodies the dual nature of the trickster, celebrated for his ingenuity yet often navigating the moral gray areas that define his character. Through his stories, the Ashanti people explore the nuances of human behavior, using Anansi's actions to reflect on the virtues and vices that shape their community.

One of Anansi's most famous escapades is his clever acquisition of all stories from the sky god, Nyame. In this tale, Anansi sets out to buy the stories that Nyame holds, but the sky god presents him with an impossible challenge: capture Onini the python, Osebo the leopard, Mmoatia the fairy, and Mmoboro the hornet. Anansi, undeterred, employs his trickery to capture each creature. For Onini, he debates the python's length, eventually tying it to a branch. He outsmarts Osebo by trapping the leopard in a deep hole filled with webs. With cunning, he convinces Mmoboro the hornet to take refuge in a calabash, and captures Mmoatia using a sticky doll. Each trick highlights Anansi's mastery of cunning and strategy, culminating in his triumphant return to Nyame with the captives. The sky god, impressed, grants Anansi the stories, which become known as "spider stories," a testament to his cleverness and tenacity.

In another tale, Anansi's greed becomes his downfall, showcasing the folly of selfishness. This story, involving the pot of wisdom, sees Anansi attempting to hoard all the wisdom in the world for himself. He places it in a pot, planning to hide it at the top of a tall tree. As he climbs, the pot, tied awkwardly to his front, hinders his progress. Anansi's son, observing his father's struggle, suggests placing the pot on his back. Frustrated that even a child possesses wisdom, Anansi throws the pot in anger, scattering its contents to the world. This tale serves as a poignant reminder that wisdom is not meant to be hoarded; it thrives when shared, reflecting Anansi's complex role as both a teacher and a cautionary figure.

Anansi's adventures also offer lessons in hospitality and fairness. In the story of Anansi and the turtle, Anansi invites Turtle to dinner but tricks him by continuously washing his hands, causing Turtle to miss the meal. Later, Turtle returns the favor, inviting Anansi to an underwater feast. Anansi, unable to stay underwater, misses out. Through this tale, the Ashanti people explore the themes of reciprocity and fairness, using Anansi's trickery to illustrate the importance of treating others as one wishes to be treated.

The symbolism associated with Anansi is as intricate as the webs he weaves. The spider, a symbol of creativity and cunning, reflects Anansi's ability to craft narratives that captivate and educate. His web, representing interconnectedness and strategy, is a metaphor for the complex relationships and stories that bind communities together. In Ashanti art and cultural expressions, Anansi is often depicted weaving his web, a visual representation of his role as the keeper of stories and the architect of cultural wisdom. His presence in storytelling traditions extends beyond folklore, influencing contemporary media and cultural narratives.

Anansi's influence is far-reaching, permeating Caribbean and African-American folklore with stories that adapt and evolve across cultures. In literature, comics, and television, Anansi's tales are retold and reimagined, keeping his spirit alive in modern narratives. His stories offer rich material for educational programs and storytelling festivals, where audiences engage with the timeless lessons and humor embedded in his adventures. Through these adaptations, Anansi continues to inspire creativity and reflection, his tales a bridge connecting past and present, reminding us of the enduring power of storytelling.

LEGBA: THE FON TRICKSTER AND GUARDIAN OF CROSSROADS

In the vibrant tapestry of Fon mythology, Legba stands as a figure of profound complexity, a trickster endowed with the ability to open and close pathways. He is the guardian of crossroads, a place where decisions are made and destinies are forged. Imagine standing at a crossroads, the paths before you shrouded in mystery. This is Legba's domain, where he holds the keys to both guidance and mischief. As a conduit for communication between the divine and human realms, Legba's role is pivotal. He serves as the bridge that spans the gap between worlds, ensuring that messages and offerings make their way to the gods. Yet, his dual nature means he is not always straightforward; sometimes, he is a helper, pointing the way forward, while at others, he is a deceiver, laying traps that test the character and integrity of those he encounters.

Legba's tales are as varied as they are instructive, each one a lesson wrapped in layers of wit and wisdom. Consider the story of Legba and the farmer, where Legba decides to teach a lesson on the importance of gratitude. The farmer, blessed with a bountiful harvest, neglects to thank Legba, who had ensured the rains came at the right time. In response, Legba withholds the rains the following season, prompting the farmer to seek his forgiveness. This story underscores the value of acknowledging the forces that aid us, a reminder to show appreciation for the blessings we receive. In another tale, Legba becomes a master of miscommunication. He relays messages between the gods, but his mischievous nature leads him to alter the messages just enough to create confusion. This results in a series of misunderstandings among the gods, which Legba eventually resolves, restoring harmony. Through this narrative, we learn about the importance of clarity and honesty in communication and how missteps can lead to chaos if not corrected.

The myth of Legba and the stolen offerings further illustrates his cunning. When a village is plagued by mysterious thefts, Legba decides to intervene. He devises a plan that involves setting a trap with a simple snare, catching the thief in the act. As the villagers watch, Legba reveals the culprit, teaching them a lesson on honesty and the futility of deceit. In doing so, Legba reinforces the moral codes that bind the community, using his trickery to uphold justice. These stories are not just entertainment; they are reflections of the values and ethics that shape the Fon people, with Legba as the guiding force.

In Fon art and iconography, Legba is often depicted with symbols that speak to his power and influence. The crossroads, a potent symbol in his mythology, represents decision and opportunity. It is where choices are made and paths are chosen, embodying the complexity of life's journey. Legba is frequently portrayed with keys and locks, representing access and control over passageways. These symbols highlight his role as a gatekeeper, one who holds the power to open doors and guide travelers along their paths. In artistic representations, Legba may be shown as an old and wise figure, his presence commanding respect and reverence.

In Vodou and related practices, Legba's influence is profound, his presence invoked in ceremonies and rituals that seek his guidance and protection. In Vodou, he is known as Papa Legba, the one who stands at the spiritual crossroads, facilitating communication with the divine. Ceremonies dedicated to Legba often involve offerings of food, drink, and other symbolic items, each chosen for its significance in connecting with the spirit world. Prayers and chants call upon Legba to open the gates, allowing for the free flow of energy and communication. His role in spiritual guidance is crucial, as he is believed to provide protection and insight to those who seek his aid. Through these practices, Legba's legacy endures, a testament to his enduring power and influence. His stories and symbols continue to inspire and guide, reminding us of the choices we make and the paths we travel.

HARE: THE CLEVER TRICKSTER IN SOUTHERN AFRICAN FOLKTALES

In the shadows of the African bush, where stories flicker like fireflies in the night, Hare emerges as a figure of intrigue and cunning. Known for his quick thinking and unmatched cleverness, Hare is a central character in Southern African folklore. His tales are woven with threads of humor and wit, each one a testament to his dual nature as both hero and deceiver. Hare's antics are legendary, serving as cautionary tales and sources of wisdom for those who listen. Through his stories, Hare teaches moral lessons that resonate across generations, offering insights into the complexities of human behavior. He embodies the spirit of adaptability and resourcefulness, traits that have endeared him to storytellers and audiences alike. In a world where strength and power often prevail, Hare shows that intelligence and ingenuity can level the playing field, turning the tables on those who underestimate him.

One of the most celebrated tales of Hare's trickery is the story of Hare and the lion. In this narrative, Hare finds himself in a precarious situation, face-to-face with a lion intent on making him a meal. Rather than succumbing to fear, Hare uses his wits to outsmart the lion, convincing him to close his eyes and count to a hundred while Hare supposedly fetches him a meal. By the time the lion realizes he's been duped, Hare is long gone, safe and sound. This tale highlights the theme of wit overcoming brute strength, a common motif in Hare's stories. It reinforces the idea that intelligence and quick thinking can be powerful tools in the face of adversity, encouraging listeners to value these traits in their own lives.

Another classic tale involves Hare and the Tortoise. Most know the fable as Aesop told it. While the African version begins and ends the same way, how the tortoise wins and the overall moral are different. In this story, Hare, confident to the point of arrogance in his speed, challenges Tortoise to a race, certain of his victory. In the African version, Hare taunts and teases Tortoise daily until the race. Tortoise gathers all his friends and relatives and hatches a plan.

When the race begins, Hare speeds forward and stops after a while to look back. Tortoise is not behind him. When Hare looks forward, he's shocked to find Tortoise ahead of him. This happens several more times until Hare reaches the finish line only to find Tortoise has already crossed the finish line despite his passing him moments before.

Aesop's narrative reminds us that slow and steady can indeed win the race, teaching the value of determination and consistency over arrogance and haste. However, the African version teaches the importance of family, community, and cooperation. Both teach morals that echo through time, reflecting the universal truth that persistence and teamwork often triumph over initial advantage.

Hare's cunning is further showcased in the tale of Hare and the farmer's crops. In this story, Hare devises a plan to access the farmer's bountiful fields, outsmarting the farmer with a series of clever tricks. However, his actions come with consequences, as the farmer eventually catches on and sets a trap for Hare. In the end, Hare's cleverness saves him once more, allowing him to escape unscathed. This tale illustrates the balance between cleverness and retribution, highlighting the importance of considering the consequences of one's actions. Through Hare's escapades, listeners are encouraged to reflect on their own choices and the potential outcomes they may face.

In Southern African art and cultural expressions, Hare is often depicted as a symbol of agility and intelligence. His portrayal captures the essence of his character, celebrating his ability to adapt and thrive in various situations. Hare's tricks and antics are not just stories; they are reflections of the values and beliefs that define the communities that tell them. In this way, Hare serves as a bridge between the past and present, his tales continuing to inspire and entertain.

Hare's influence extends beyond folklore, permeating modern culture in various forms. His stories are a staple in Southern African literature, where they are retold and reimagined for new audiences. Educational programs and storytelling festivals celebrate

Hare's legacy, using his tales as a tool for moral education and cultural preservation. Through these venues, Hare's stories continue to live on, offering timeless lessons that resonate with listeners of all ages. Hare's presence in modern media ensures that his legacy endures, reminding us of the power of storytelling to connect us to our cultural heritage.

As we wrap up our exploration of trickster archetypes, we see how these figures, from Eshu to Hare, reveal the diverse ways cultures use mythology to explore complex ideas. Their stories are not just about cunning and deceit but also about the human experience—our struggles, our triumphs, our ability to overcome challenges through creativity and wit. This rich tapestry of tales invites us to reflect on our own lives, our choices, and the lessons we pass on.

CHAPTER 7: COMPARATIVE MYTHOLOGICAL ANALYSIS: THEMES OF FERTILITY AND AGRICULTURE

Themes of fertility and agriculture are central to many mythologies, representing the life-giving forces that sustain communities and ensure their prosperity. In African mythology, deities associated with fertility and agriculture embody the nurturing and transformative power of nature. This chapter explores four significant African deities: Oshun of the Yoruba, Mbokomu of the Ngombe, Modjadji of the Lovedu, and Nyame of the Ashanti. Each of these deities plays a vital role in the fertility and agricultural cycles of their respective cultures, providing insights into the importance of growth, renewal, and the interconnectedness of life.

Oshun, the Yoruba goddess of fertility and rivers, is a beacon of abundance and love. Her influence extends beyond the physical realm, nurturing both the land and the hearts of her people. As the goddess of rivers, Oshun ensures the fertility of the earth, her waters sustaining crops and nourishing the soil. Her connection to love and motherhood further emphasizes her role in community growth and unity. Oshun's myths, such as the creation of rivers from her tears, highlight her role as a nurturer, turning sorrow into renewal and ensuring the prosperity of her people.

Mbokomu, the first woman and gardener in Ngombe mythology, embodies fertility and agriculture in Central Africa. Her influence is deeply connected to the earth, guiding the cycles of planting and harvest. Mbokomu's nurturing spirit transforms barren soil into fields of plenty, ensuring that her people have the sustenance they need to thrive. Her stories emphasize her role as a protector of the land and a guardian of family and community well-being. Through her guidance, farmers learn to work in harmony with the natural cycles, celebrating the interconnectedness of life and the earth.

Modjadji, the Rain Queen of the Lovedu people, wields the power to summon rain, transforming the land and ensuring agricultural success. Her influence over weather patterns is crucial to the fertility of the earth, and her rainmaking abilities sustain crops and provide life to the community. Modjadji's myths portray her as a compassionate figure who brings life to the parched earth, her connection to the natural world ensuring the prosperity of her people. The Lovedu people look to her as both a protector and provider, her presence a reminder of the delicate balance between humanity and nature.

Nyame, the sky god of the Ashanti, is a powerful figure who controls the elements that sustain life. His influence over the sun and rain ensures the fertility of the land, and his presence is felt in every drop of rain and ray of sunlight. Nyame's myths highlight his role as a provider, his actions ensuring that the land remains fertile and the people prosperous. His teachings offer insight into the balance between human effort and divine order, guiding the Ashanti people in their agricultural practices and helping them align with the natural rhythms of the earth.

These four deities—Oshun, Mbokomu, Modjadji, and Nyame—represent the vital forces of fertility and agriculture, each playing a unique role in sustaining their communities. Through their stories, we gain a deeper understanding of the interconnectedness of life, the importance of growth and renewal, and the delicate balance between humanity and nature. The myths of these deities remind us that the forces of fertility and agriculture are not merely physical processes but are deeply spiritual, shaping the lives and cultures of those who honor them.

As we explore these myths, we are invited to reflect on our own relationship with the natural world and the cycles of growth and renewal that sustain us. These deities embody the nurturing power of nature, encouraging us to live in harmony with the earth and to recognize the profound connections that bind us all. Through their stories, we find inspiration to cultivate not only the land but also the relationships and values that sustain our communities, ensuring a future of abundance and prosperity.

OSHUN: GODDESS OF FERTILITY AND ABUNDANCE

In the heart of Yoruba tradition, where the rivers wind through lush landscapes and the air hums with life, Oshun stands as a beacon of fertility and abundance. Picture a serene river, its waters glistening under the sun, flowing with a quiet strength that nurtures everything it touches. This is Oshun, the goddess who commands the rivers and freshwater bodies, bringing life to the land and its people. Her influence extends beyond the physical realm, reaching into the hearts of those who seek her blessings for fertility, childbirth, and motherhood. Oshun is not just a deity of the waters; she is a symbol of love and attraction, fostering growth within communities by uniting hearts and nurturing the bonds of family.

Oshun's role in Yoruba mythology is profound, her presence felt in every ripple of water and every heartbeat of love. As the goddess of fertility, she is revered for her ability to bring forth life, ensuring that the land remains fertile and bountiful. Her connection to the rivers makes her a vital force in agricultural success, as these waterways are the lifelines that sustain crops and nourish the soil. When the rains fall, it is Oshun's tears that quench the earth's thirst, a poignant reminder of her enduring presence and care. Her influence on childbirth and motherhood further underscores her role as a guardian of life, offering comfort and guidance to those on the journey to parenthood. In the complex tapestry of Yoruba beliefs, Oshun's connection to love and attraction fosters community growth, as her blessings encourage unity and cooperation among the people.

The myths that surround Oshun are as vibrant as the goddess herself, each one a testament to her power and compassion. One such story tells of Oshun's tears, which, when shed, create the rivers that nourish the land. In this tale, her tears are not a sign of sorrow but of joy and renewal, a gift to the earth that ensures its continued prosperity. Another myth speaks of Oshun blessing barren women with children, her touch transforming despair into hope as she grants the gift of life. These stories illustrate Oshun's deep connection to fertility, highlighting her role as a nurturer and protector. Her involvement in the annual Ifa divination rituals is a further testament to her importance. These ceremonies call upon her wisdom to ensure agricultural success and community well-being. Through these narratives, Oshun emerges as a multifaceted figure, embodying the complex interplay of love, life, and renewal.

In the symbolism associated with Oshun, we find a rich tapestry of meanings that reflect her diverse attributes. The river is a powerful symbol of life and sustenance, representing the flow of energy and the cycle of renewal that Oshun embodies. In rituals, honey, gold, and mirrors hold particular significance, each element chosen for its connection to Oshun's essence. Honey, with its golden hue and sweet taste, symbolizes the sweetness of life and the nourishment that Oshun provides. Gold, a precious metal, reflects her beauty and radiance, while mirrors serve as a portal to self-reflection and inner wisdom. In Yoruba art and iconography, Oshun is often depicted with these symbols, her image a celebration of her timeless beauty and her enduring influence on the world.

Take a moment to reflect on Oshun's role in your life. How do her stories and symbols resonate with you? Consider the ways in which her presence might inspire growth and renewal in your own journey. Write down your thoughts, exploring the connections between Oshun's mythology and your personal experiences.

The rituals and practices that honor Oshun are vibrant expressions of faith and gratitude, reflecting the deep reverence the Yoruba people hold for their beloved goddess. The Oshun-Osogbo Festival, held annually, is a time of joyous celebration, drawing devotees from far and wide to pay homage at the sacred river. Participants gather at the Osun-Osogbo Sacred Grove, a UNESCO World Heritage site, where the air is filled with song and the scent of offerings. Common offerings to Oshun include sweet foods, fresh water, and other items that symbolize abundance and gratitude. Priestesses play a vital role in these ceremonies, leading the community in prayers and rituals that seek Oshun's blessings and favor. Through these practices, the bonds between the people and Oshun are strengthened, ensuring that her legacy continues to inspire and guide future generations.

MBOKOMU: THE CENTRAL AFRICAN FERTILITY DEITY

In the rich and verdant landscapes of Central Africa, the presence of Mbokomu is as profound as the earth beneath your feet. She is the goddess who embodies fertility, agriculture, and the nurturing spirit of the land. As the first woman and the first gardener in Ngombe mythology, Mbokomu's influence extends deep into the soil, guiding the cycles of planting and harvest. Her role as a fertility deity is not just symbolic; it is a living, breathing connection to the Earth and its bounties. Mbokomu's nurturing nature ensures that crops flourish, delivering the sustenance and prosperity that communities rely on. Her protective qualities are like the embrace of a mother, watching over the soil and ensuring the land remains fertile and life-sustaining. In her hands, the Earth becomes a garden, where life begins and thrives, nourishing both body and spirit.

The stories of Mbokomu are imbued with themes of abundance and care, each illustrating her pivotal role in Central African mythology. One legend recounts how Mbokomu blessed the land with bountiful harvests, her touch transforming barren soil into fields of plenty. It is said that where she walked, the Earth bloomed with life, a testament to her power and grace. In another tale, Mbokomu aids women in childbirth, her wisdom guiding them through the miracle of bringing new life into the world. Her presence provides comfort and strength, ensuring safe deliveries and healthy children. These stories highlight her deep connection to motherhood, reflecting her role as a guardian of family and community well-being. Mbokomu's guidance extends to farmers, whom she instructs in the rhythms of planting and harvest, teaching them to work in harmony with the Earth's natural cycles. Through these narratives, Mbokomu's impact on fertility and agriculture is celebrated, her influence shaping the lives of those who honor her.

In the symbolism surrounding Mbokomu, the Earth and plants hold a special place, representing the life-giving and nurturing aspects of her being. The Earth is her domain, a symbol of fertility and growth, where seeds are sown and nurtured into life. Plants, with their vibrant colors and diverse forms, embody the beauty and potential of the natural world. In rituals, seeds, and agricultural tools are used as objects of worship, each item chosen for its significance in connecting with Mbokomu's essence. These symbols serve as reminders of her presence and her role as the steward of the land. In Central African art and iconography, Mbokomu is often depicted with these symbols, her image a celebration of her timeless beauty and enduring influence on the world. Her representation is not just an artistic expression; it is a testament to the reverence and gratitude that her followers hold for her.

The rituals and practices dedicated to Mbokomu are vibrant celebrations of life and abundance, reflecting the deep respect and devotion that the Central African people have for their beloved goddess. Common rituals involve offerings of seeds, fruits, and soil, symbolic acts that honor Mbokomu's role in the cycle of growth and renewal. These offerings are made at sacred sites, such as fields and gardens, where her presence is believed to be strongest. Traditional healers and priests play a crucial role in these practices, acting as intermediaries between the earthly and the divine. Their chants and prayers reach out to Mbokomu, inviting her presence and blessing. Annual festivals and celebrations dedicated to Mbokomu are a time of joy and renewal, gatherings that bring the community together in shared homage. These events are marked by music, dance, and storytelling, creating an atmosphere of unity and reverence. Through these practices, the relationship between humans and Mbokomu is honored and maintained, ensuring that her legacy continues to inspire and guide future generations.

MODJADJI: THE RAIN QUEEN AND AGRICULTURAL PROSPERITY IN SOUTHERN AFRICA

Imagine the skies darkening, heavy with the promise of rain as the air thickens with anticipation. At the heart of South African mythology stands Modjadji, the Rain Queen, whose very presence commands the weather. She wields the power to summon rain, transforming barren lands into fields of plenty. Her influence over weather patterns is legendary, and her ability to control the rains ensures that the crops flourish and the earth remains fertile. Modjadji's role goes beyond mere weather control; she embodies fertility and the health of the land, a living testament to the interconnectedness of nature and community. Her connection to the earth is profound, and her rainmaking abilities are a vital force in sustaining agricultural cycles and ensuring bountiful harvests. The Lovedu people, in their reverence, look to her as both a protector and provider, her presence a constant reminder of the delicate balance between humanity and nature.

The myths surrounding Modjadji paint her as a powerful and compassionate figure, revered for her ability to bring life to the parched earth. One such tale tells of a time when drought gripped the land, the fields withering under the relentless sun. It was Modjadji who, with a wave of her hand, called forth the rains, her connection to the heavens ensuring the survival of her people. Her rainmaking abilities are not just a skill but a sacred duty, a responsibility she embraces with grace and wisdom. Another story speaks of her guidance to the Lovedu people in agricultural practices, her insights into the rhythms of nature helping them to plant and harvest in harmony with the seasons. In these narratives, Modjadji's impact is profound, her influence shaping the lives and livelihoods of those who honor her. Her presence is felt in every drop of rain, her spirit woven into the fabric of the land.

The symbols associated with Modjadji are rich with meaning, each a reflection of her enduring power and grace. Rain, in its life-giving essence, is a potent symbol of renewal and rebirth, embodying the cycles of nature that Modjadji governs. In her worship, ritual objects such as water vessels and rain stones hold particular significance, each item chosen for its connection to her divine influence. These objects are not merely ceremonial; they are sacred tools that facilitate communication with the Rain Queen, inviting her presence and blessing. In South African art and cultural expressions, Modjadji is often depicted with these symbols, her image a celebration of her beauty and power. The imagery of rain and water permeates these artistic traditions, capturing the dynamic and nurturing aspects of her nature. Through these symbols, Modjadji's legacy endures, and her influence is felt in every facet of life.

The rituals and practices dedicated to Modjadji are vibrant expressions of faith and devotion, reflecting the deep reverence the Lovedu people hold for their Rain Queen. Annual rainmaking ceremonies are a time of celebration and renewal, drawing the community together in shared homage. During these events, offerings of water and agricultural produce are made with reverence, each item a token of gratitude and respect. The royal family and traditional healers play a central role in these practices, their presence ensuring that the rituals are carried out with the dignity they deserve. Their involvement underscores the deep connection between Modjadji and the community, a bond that is both spiritual and cultural. Through these practices, the relationship between the Lovedu people and Modjadji is honored and maintained, ensuring that her legacy continues to inspire and guide future generations. Like the rain she brings, her story is a source of life and renewal, a reminder of the power of nature and the enduring spirit of the land.

NYAME: THE ASHANTI SKY GOD AND AGRICULTURAL CYCLES

Nyame, the revered sky god of the Ashanti people, is a figure of immense power and significance. Imagine the vast expanse of the sky, an endless canvas painted with the hues of sunrise and sunset. This is Nyame's domain, where he orchestrates the patterns of the sun and rain, weaving them into the fabric of life. As the master of weather patterns, Nyame's influence extends to the very heart of agriculture, ensuring that the land remains fertile and the crops thrive. His control over the elements is absolute; the sun warms the earth under his watchful eye, while the rain falls at his command, nourishing the soil and nurturing the seeds that grow into sustenance for the Ashanti people. Nyame's presence is felt in every drop of rain and every ray of sunlight, a testament to his role as the guardian of fertility and prosperity. His connection to the land is profound, and his blessings ensure that the cycles of growth and renewal continue unabated.

The myths surrounding Nyame are rich with tales of his benevolence and power. One such story tells of a time when the land was parched and the people despaired for lack of rain. In their need, they turned to Nyame, who heard their pleas and sent rain to drench the earth, ensuring a good harvest. This myth highlights Nyame's role as a provider. His actions ensure that the land remains fertile and the people prosperous. Another tale describes his blessing of the soil, a divine touch that transforms barren ground into fields of abundance. In these stories, Nyame's influence is evident; his presence ensures that the Ashanti people have the resources they need to thrive. Through his guidance, they learn the rhythms of planting and harvesting, aligning their efforts with the natural cycles that Nyame oversees. His teachings are a source of wisdom, offering insight into the balance between human endeavor and the divine order.

In the symbolism associated with Nyame, the sky and celestial bodies hold a special place, representing his power and authority. With its life-giving warmth, the sun is a potent symbol of Nyame's influence, a reminder of his role in sustaining life. In rituals, objects such as sun disks and rain symbols are used to honor Nyame, each item chosen for its connection to his divine essence. These symbols are not mere decorations; they are sacred tools that facilitate communication with the sky god, inviting his presence and blessing. In Ashanti art and cultural expressions, Nyame is often depicted with these celestial symbols, his image a celebration of his majesty and power. The imagery of the sky and its wonders permeates these artistic traditions, capturing the awe and reverence that Nyame inspires. Through these symbols, his legacy endures, and his influence is felt in every aspect of life.

The rituals and practices dedicated to Nyame are vibrant expressions of faith and gratitude, reflecting the Ashanti people's deep reverence for their sky god. Annual harvest festivals are a time of celebration and thanksgiving, gatherings that bring the community together in shared homage. During these events, offerings of crops and symbolic objects are made with reverence, each item a token of gratitude and respect. Priests and community leaders play a central role in these practices, their presence ensuring that the rituals are carried out with the dignity they deserve. Their involvement underscores the deep connection between Nyame and the community, a bond that is both spiritual and cultural. Through these practices, the relationship between the Ashanti people and Nyame is honored and maintained, ensuring that his legacy continues to inspire and guide future generations. Like the sky itself, his story is a source of wonder and inspiration, a reminder of the power of nature and the enduring spirit of the land.

As we reflect on these stories and symbols, we see how Nyame's influence permeates the lives of those who honor him. His role in the cycles of fertility and agriculture is not just a myth; it is a living presence that continues to shape the Ashanti people and their connection to the land. Through Nyame's guidance, they find balance and harmony, learning to work in harmony with the natural world and the divine forces that sustain it. His story is a testament to the enduring power of faith and tradition, a reminder that the lessons of the past continue to inform and inspire the present. As we conclude this chapter, we turn our gaze to new horizons, where the stories of other deities await, each one a thread in the rich tapestry of African mythology.

YORUBA   KONGO   ZULU

CHAPTER 8: THE CONCEPT OF THE AFTERLIFE IN AFRICAN BELIEFS

The concept of the afterlife is a profound and integral part of African spiritual beliefs, reflecting the deep connection between the living and the spiritual realms. In African cultures, death is not seen as an end but as a transition to another phase of existence, where the soul continues its journey. This chapter explores the concepts of the afterlife in the beliefs of four African cultures: the Yoruba, the Akan, the Igbo, and the Zulu. Each of these cultures offers a unique perspective on the afterlife, emphasizing the importance of ancestors, community, and spiritual continuity.

In Yoruba belief, the afterlife is a vibrant continuation of existence, where the ancestors dwell in Orun, the heavenly abode. These ancestors are not distant or disconnected; they actively watch over and guide the living, serving as intermediaries between humans and the divine. Ancestor worship is central to Yoruba spirituality, with rituals and offerings ensuring that the spirits remain at peace and continue to protect their descendants. The Egungun festival is a significant event that honors the ancestors, with elaborate masquerades bringing the spirits to life and reaffirming the bond between the living and the departed. The Babalawo, a spiritual guide, plays a crucial role in maintaining this connection, using divination to communicate with the ancestors and offer guidance to the community.

The Akan people of Ghana also hold a deep belief in the afterlife, viewing it as a journey to Asamando, the land of the ancestors. In Akan cosmology, death is a passage to a realm where the soul joins the ancestors, who are revered as guardians of the family and community. The living maintain a strong relationship with their ancestors through libations, prayers, and offerings, seeking their blessings and protection. The belief in the afterlife shapes Akan funeral practices, which are elaborate ceremonies designed to ensure a smooth transition for the deceased. These rituals emphasize the importance of honoring the dead and maintaining harmony between the physical and spiritual worlds.

In Igbo culture, the afterlife is known as Ala Mmụọ, the land of the spirits. The Igbo believe that the dead continue to exist in a spiritual realm, where they watch over their families and influence the living world. Ancestors are seen as vital members of the community, and their favor is sought through rituals and offerings. The concept of "ndichie," or ancestral spirits, is central to Igbo spirituality, with the ancestors serving as custodians of moral values and traditions. The Igbo also believe in reincarnation, where the souls of the departed return to the physical world through new births, continuing the cycle of life and maintaining the connection between generations.

The Zulu people of Southern Africa believe in an afterlife where the spirits of the ancestors, known as Amadlozi or Abaphansi, play an active role in the lives of the living. The Zulu view death as a transition to the spiritual realm, where the ancestors become protectors and guides for their descendants. Communication with the ancestors is maintained through rituals, offerings, and the guidance of traditional healers, known as sangomas. The Zulu believe that the ancestors have the power to influence events in the physical world, providing blessings, protection, and guidance. The concept of the afterlife is deeply intertwined with Zulu social and cultural practices, emphasizing the importance of family, community, and respect for those who have passed on.

These four cultures—Yoruba, Akan, Igbo, and Zulu—offer rich and diverse perspectives on the afterlife, each highlighting the enduring connection between the living and the spiritual realms. Through their beliefs and practices, we see a common thread: the reverence for ancestors, the importance of maintaining harmony between the physical and spiritual worlds, and the understanding that death is not an end but a continuation of the soul's journey. The afterlife in African belief systems is not a distant or abstract concept; it is a living reality, one that shapes the values, rituals, and daily lives of those who honor it.

As we explore these beliefs, we are invited to reflect on our own understanding of life, death, and the connections that bind us across generations. The African concepts of the afterlife remind us of the importance of community, the wisdom of those who came before us, and the enduring nature of the human spirit. Through these traditions, we find inspiration to honor our own ancestors and to recognize the profound continuity of life that transcends the boundaries of the physical world.

THE REALMS OF THE YORUBA AFTERLIFE

The evening air in a Yoruba village is often filled with the scent of incense and the sound of rhythmic drumming. As the sun sets, families gather, their faces glowing in the warm light of flickering candles. This is a time for reflection and connection, a moment to reach beyond the veil that separates the living from the spiritual realm. Like many African cultures, the Yoruba hold a deep belief in the continuation of the soul after death. For them, the afterlife is not a distant concept but a vibrant, living reality. It is a realm where the ancestors dwell, a place where their spirits continue to watch over and guide their descendants. This belief is woven into the fabric of daily life, influencing everything from family dynamics to community rituals.

In Yoruba cosmology, the afterlife is divided into two realms: Orun, the heavenly abode, and Aiye, the earthly plane. Orun is a place of spiritual fulfillment where the ancestors reside, keeping a watchful eye on the world below. These ancestors are not just distant figures; they are active participants in the lives of their living relatives. They serve as intermediaries between the divine and the earthly, bridging the gap between humans and the gods. This relationship is reciprocal, as the living honor their ancestors through rituals and offerings, ensuring that their spirits remain at peace. It's a connection that transcends time and space, uniting generations in a shared spiritual journey.

Ancestor worship is a cornerstone of Yoruba tradition, a practice rich with symbolism and meaning. Ceremonies to honor the ancestors are carefully crafted, often involving offerings of food, drink, and personal items. These gifts are not mere tokens; they are acts of devotion and expressions of gratitude for the guidance and protection the ancestors provide. The annual Egungun festival is a particularly significant event, a vibrant celebration of the spirits of the deceased. During the festival, elaborate masquerades and dances bring the ancestors to life, their presence felt in the rhythmic movements and pulsating drumbeats. The community comes together in joyous reverence, reaffirming their connection to those who have gone before.

Central to these practices is the Babalawo, the priest and spiritual guide who facilitates communication with the ancestors. The Babalawo is a respected figure entrusted with the sacred duty of interpreting the will of the spirits. Through divination and ritual, he offers insights and counsel, helping the community navigate the challenges of life. His role is one of both mediator and protector, ensuring that the spiritual balance is maintained. In this way, the connection to the ancestors is not just a matter of faith but a living relationship, one that is nurtured and sustained through ongoing dialogue and ritual.

The symbolism of ancestor worship in Yoruba culture is profound, reflecting deep-seated values and beliefs. Ancestors are seen as protectors and guides. Their wisdom and experience are a source of strength for the living. They embody the continuity of life, a reminder that each generation is part of a larger tapestry. This understanding is vividly expressed through the use of masks and costumes in Egungun rituals. These masks are not mere disguises; they are sacred artifacts, believed to house the spirits of the ancestors during the festival. Each mask is meticulously crafted, its design reflecting the lineage and identity of the wearer. Through these rituals, the ancestors are made present, their presence a tangible force within the community.

Food, drink, and other offerings play a crucial role in these ceremonies, serving as a bridge between the physical and spiritual worlds. These offerings are chosen with care, each item imbued with symbolic meaning. Food represents sustenance and nourishment, while drink symbolizes the flow of life and spirit. Together, they form a language of reverence, a way for the living to communicate their respect and devotion. By honoring the ancestors in this way, the Yoruba ensure that their spirits remain vibrant and engaged, a vital part of the community's spiritual life.

The narratives and myths surrounding the Yoruba afterlife are rich with wisdom and insight, offering a window into the cultural beliefs that shape this understanding. One such story is the myth of Orunmila, the deity of wisdom, who guides souls to the afterlife. Orunmila is a benevolent figure, a guardian of the spiritual journey who ensures that each soul finds its rightful place in Orun. His presence is a source of comfort and assurance, a reminder that the afterlife is not an end but a continuation of the soul's journey. Other stories speak of ancestors intervening in the lives of the living, offering guidance and protection in times of need. These tales highlight the moral conduct expected of individuals, emphasizing the importance of living a life of integrity and honor.

In Yoruba belief, the journey to Orun is influenced by one's actions and choices in life. Moral conduct is not just a personal matter; it's a communal responsibility, one that reflects the values and ethics of the society as a whole. By living according to these principles, individuals ensure not only their own spiritual fulfillment but also the well-being of their community. This understanding is woven into the fabric of Yoruba culture, a testament to the enduring power of the ancestors and their role in shaping the lives of their descendants.

THE KONGO BELIEF IN THE KALUNGA LINE

Imagine a landscape where the horizon is not just a line but a bridge connecting two realms. For the Kongo people, the Kalunga line serves as this boundary, a spiritual division between the world of the living and the world of the dead. It's more than just a metaphor; it's a gateway separating life from the afterlife, a place both feared and revered. This line is not visible to the eye but is felt in the heart and spirit. Beyond this boundary lies Mpemba, the land of the dead, where ancestors reside. They are not ghosts of the past but vibrant spirits who continue to influence the living world. Water, with its fluidity and depth, is often seen as the passage between these realms. Rivers and oceans become portals, their currents carrying souls across the Kalunga line. This belief reflects a deep understanding of water's dual nature—nurturing yet powerful, grounding yet transcendent.

Rituals in the Kongo culture focus on helping souls navigate this transition. Funerary rites are more than ceremonial; they are essential to ensure that the soul journeys safely to Mpemba. Every step of the burial process holds meaning. The body is prepared with care, wrapped in cloth that symbolizes the embrace of the earth. Offerings are made, not just to honor the deceased but to provide them with the tools they need for their journey. These offerings might include food, drink, and personal items that held significance in life. Nkisi, spiritual objects imbued with protective power, are often placed with the deceased. These objects, created by skilled artisans, serve as guides and protectors, ensuring that the path to Mpemba is clear and unobstructed.

The Nganga, or spiritual healer, plays a pivotal role in these practices. They are the keepers of ancient wisdom, trained in the ways of the spirit world. Their knowledge of herbs, chants, and rituals helps guide the soul, acting as both a map and a beacon. Through their ceremonies, the Nganga communicates with the ancestors, seeking their blessing and guidance. This relationship is reciprocal, as the ancestors offer protection and insight in return. The Nganga's role is crucial, for they ensure that the spiritual balance is maintained, allowing the living to honor their dead and the dead to watch over the living.

The Kalunga line holds profound significance in Kongo spirituality. It symbolizes transition and transformation, a reminder that life and death are not opposites but part of a continuum. This understanding is reflected in the rituals that mark life's milestones, from birth to death and beyond. Rivers and oceans, with their endless flow, are central to these rituals. They represent the cycle of life, the eternal journey of the soul. Water is used in ceremonies to cleanse and purify, to connect the physical with the spiritual. It is both a barrier and a bridge, a force that both separates and unites.

Mirrors and other reflective surfaces are also used in Kongo spiritual practices. They serve as portals, allowing glimpses into the world beyond the Kalunga line. By gazing into a mirror, one might catch a reflection of the spirit world, a fleeting image of what lies beyond. These reflections are considered sacred, a means of communicating with the ancestors. They remind the living of their connection to the past, to the spirits who guide and protect them. Through these symbols, the Kongo people maintain a deep and abiding relationship with their ancestors, one that transcends the boundaries of life and death.

The myths surrounding the Kongo afterlife are rich with narrative and meaning. One of the most revered is the myth of Nzambi Mpungu, the supreme deity who guides souls across the Kalunga line. This story speaks of a compassionate god who ensures that every soul finds its place in Mpemba. Nzambi Mpungu is not just a distant figure; he is a guardian and a guide, a presence felt in the quiet moments of reflection and the grand ceremonies of passage. Other stories tell of ancestors who reach back across the Kalunga line to aid their living descendants. They offer wisdom, protection, and guidance, ensuring that the community remains strong and united.

The journey to the afterlife is influenced by one's actions and choices in life. Moral conduct is not just a personal matter but a reflection of communal values. Living a life of integrity, honor, and respect ensures a peaceful passage to Mpemba. This belief is woven into the fabric of Kongo culture, reminding individuals of their responsibilities to themselves, their community, and their ancestors. Through these stories and beliefs, the Kongo people honor their past while embracing the present, ensuring that the cycle of life continues unbroken.

THE ZULU AFTERLIFE: ANCESTRAL SPIRITS AND THE SPIRIT WORLD

In the heart of Zulu belief lies a profound respect for the ancestors, known as the Amadlozi, who reside in the spirit world. This realm is not an abstract concept but a vibrant extension of the living world, where the souls of the departed continue their existence. For the Zulu people, the afterlife is a place where the ancestors watch over the living, offering guidance and protection in daily life. These ancestral spirits are seen as guardians, intermediaries who mediate between the physical and spiritual realms. They hold a revered status, their wisdom accumulated over lifetimes, and their presence is felt in the lingering echoes of tradition and the quiet moments of introspection. Maintaining a connection with these spirits is not just a cultural practice but a fundamental aspect of Zulu spirituality, ensuring that the values and teachings of the past continue to guide and shape the present.

Ancestral worship among the Zulu is a rich tapestry of rituals and ceremonies, each one designed to honor the spirits and reaffirm the bonds between the living and the dead. At the heart of these practices are offerings, which are more than mere gifts; they are acts of devotion and respect. These offerings might include beer brewed specially for the occasion and portions of food set aside during meals. These items symbolize sustenance and community, reflecting the shared life between ancestors and their descendants. The annual Umkhosi Wokweshwama festival is a particularly significant event, marking the celebration of the first fruits and honoring the ancestors. During this festival, the community comes together in a vibrant expression of gratitude and remembrance, offering the first harvest to the Amadlozi as a gesture of thanks and recognition of their ongoing influence.

Central to the communication with the ancestors is the Sangoma, the traditional healer who serves as a conduit between the earthly and spiritual worlds. The Sangoma is a respected figure, steeped in knowledge and tradition, entrusted with the sacred duty of interpreting the will of the ancestors. Through rituals and divination, the Sangoma seeks to understand the messages from the spirit world, offering insights and guidance to the community. Their role is pivotal, ensuring that the spiritual balance is maintained and that the living remain attuned to the wisdom of the past. This connection is not static but a dynamic exchange, where the living seek counsel from the ancestors, and the ancestors, in turn, offer protection and support.

The symbolism of ancestral spirits in Zulu culture runs deep, reflecting the core values and beliefs of the people. Ancestors are sources of wisdom and protection, their presence a constant reminder of the enduring bond between generations. This understanding is vividly expressed through the use of cattle and other livestock in sacrificial rituals. Cattle hold a place of honor in Zulu society, symbolizing wealth, status, and community. In these rituals, the sacrifice of cattle is a profound act of reverence, a way to communicate with the ancestors and seek their favor. The meat is shared among the participants, reinforcing the sense of unity and interconnectedness that defines the Zulu way of life. Beer, too, plays a significant role in these ceremonies. Its preparation and consumption is a communal act that honors the spirits and celebrates the continuity of life.

The narratives and myths surrounding the Zulu afterlife are rich with meaning, offering insights into the beliefs that shape this understanding. One of the most revered myths is that of Unkulunkulu, the great ancestor who guides souls to the spirit world. This story speaks of a benevolent figure who ensures that each soul finds its place among the ancestors, a guardian of the spiritual journey who embodies the values of compassion and wisdom. Other tales recount the interventions of ancestors in the lives of the living, illustrating their role as protectors and guides. These stories emphasize the importance of moral conduct, highlighting the belief that one's actions and choices in life influence their journey to the spirit world. Living a life of integrity and respect ensures not only personal fulfillment but also the well-being of the community, reflecting the interconnectedness that lies at the heart of Zulu culture.

In Zulu belief, the afterlife is not an end but a continuation, a testament to the enduring power of the ancestors and their role in shaping the lives of their descendants. This understanding is woven into the fabric of Zulu society, a reminder that each generation is part of a larger story, one that transcends time and space. Through the rituals, symbols, and stories that define this belief, the Zulu people honor their past while embracing the present, ensuring that the cycle of life and spirit continues unbroken. The chapter closes, inviting reflection on these themes and setting the stage for further exploration of African spirituality in the chapters to come.

CHAPTER 9: MYTHOLOGICAL CREATURES AND BEINGS

The concept of mythical creatures and beings is a fascinating aspect of African folklore, representing the rich cultural imagination and the deep connection between the physical and spiritual realms. In African mythology, these creatures are not just figments of the imagination but powerful symbols that reflect the fears, hopes, and values of the communities that tell their stories. This chapter explores four notable mythical beings from African folklore: the Tokoloshe, Mami Wata, the Grootslang, and the Adze. Each of these beings offers unique insights into the cultural beliefs of their respective regions, highlighting themes of protection, fear, wealth, and the supernatural.

The Tokoloshe is a mischievous creature from Southern African folklore, often described as a small, dwarf-like figure capable of rendering itself invisible. Known for its playful yet troublesome antics, the Tokoloshe is both feared and respected. It is believed to sneak into households at night, causing disturbances such as rearranging furniture or hiding objects. In some stories, the Tokoloshe is summoned by witches to carry out malevolent deeds, spreading fear and chaos. Traditional healers, known as sangomas, play a crucial role in addressing Tokoloshe disturbances, using rituals and protective charms to cleanse spaces and protect individuals. The Tokoloshe serves as a cautionary figure in children's stories, embodying the struggle between order and chaos and the unseen forces that influence daily life.

Mami Wata, a powerful water spirit celebrated across West and Central Africa, embodies the mysteries and beauty of the oceans, rivers, and lakes. Often depicted as an enchanting mermaid or a stunning woman adorned with jewels, Mami Wata is associated with wealth, fertility, and seduction. Her legends tell of fishermen encountering her under the moonlit sky, where she either bestows blessings or brings misfortune based on their reverence. Mami Wata's influence extends beyond the spiritual, permeating African art and literature, where she is celebrated as a symbol of beauty and power. Rituals dedicated to Mami Wata involve offerings of perfume, jewelry, and sweet foods, each chosen for its symbolic connection to her domains. Through these practices, Mami Wata's legacy endures as a living symbol of the power and mystery of the natural world.

The Grootslang, a colossal serpent from South African mythology, is a creature of immense strength and cunning. Said to dwell in hidden caves filled with diamonds, the Grootslang is both a guardian of treasure and a symbol of danger. Legends tell of adventurers attempting to outwit the creature to claim its riches, but the Grootslang's formidable power ensures that few succeed. The Grootslang is believed to be one of the first creatures created by the gods, possessing both the strength of an elephant and the cunning of a serpent. Communities living near its supposed haunts have developed rituals to protect themselves, often involving offerings to appease the creature and maintain balance. The Grootslang's story serves as a reminder of the perils of greed and the power of the natural world.

The Adze, a vampiric spirit from Ewe folklore in Togo and Ghana, is known for its ability to transform into a firefly or other small insect. In this form, the Adze slips into homes undetected, sucking blood and spreading illness among villagers. Its presence is often associated with witchcraft and malevolent magic, casting a shadow of fear over the community. The Adze symbolizes the darker side of the supernatural, reflecting concerns about the dangers of the unknown. Traditional healers play a crucial role in combating the Adze, using rituals and protective charms to ward off its influence. The Adze's story is a cautionary tale about the thin line between the natural and supernatural, reminding people of the unseen threats that lurk in the shadows.

These four mythical beings—the Tokoloshe, Mami Wata, the Grootslang, and the Adze—offer a glimpse into the rich tapestry of African folklore, each reflecting the beliefs, fears, and values of the communities that tell their stories. Through their myths, we are invited to explore the unseen forces that shape our world, offering a window into the mysteries that lie just beneath the surface. These creatures are not merely tales of fantasy; they embody cultural truths, inviting us to reflect on the complexities of the human experience and the powerful connection between the natural and the supernatural.

As we explore these myths, we are reminded of the importance of storytelling in preserving cultural heritage and understanding the world around us. These mythical beings challenge us to consider our own fears, desires, and the balance between order and chaos. Through their stories, we find inspiration to respect the mysteries of life and to honor the deep cultural connections that bind us to the past and to each other.

TOKOLOSHE: THE TRICKSTER WITH MANY FACES

In the realm of myth and legend, where the boundaries between reality and imagination blur, creatures like the Tokoloshe emerge from the shadows. Picture a moonlit night in a Southern African village, where the air is thick with stories passed down from elders, whispered in the hush of evening. The Tokoloshe is a being that has captured the imaginations of many, often described as a small, dwarf-like figure with a mischievous glint in its eye. Known to be elusive, this creature can render itself invisible or appear only partially, leaving behind a trail of mischief and unexplained events. Its presence is often felt rather than seen, a whisper of movement or a shadow flitting across a room. The Tokoloshe's antics are the stuff of legend, causing trouble wherever it goes, much like a playful spirit with a penchant for stirring chaos.

The stories surrounding the Tokoloshe are as varied as the landscapes it inhabits. In one tale, it is said to sneak into households under the cover of night, rearranging furniture or hiding objects to confuse and frustrate the inhabitants. Imagine waking up to find your belongings in disarray, the quiet of the night interrupted by the Tokoloshe's unseen hand. Yet, its mischief can take a darker turn, with tales of the Tokoloshe being summoned by witches to carry out malevolent deeds. In this guise, it becomes an agent of chaos, spreading fear and discord at the behest of those who seek to wield its power. Legends also speak of its origins, describing how the Tokoloshe came to be—a mix of magic and folklore that has evolved over time, reflecting the fears and hopes of the people who tell its tale.

In Southern African culture, Tokoloshe holds a unique place, often serving as a cautionary figure in children's stories. Much like the boogeyman in Western folklore, it is used to instill lessons or discourage naughty behavior, a reminder of the consequences that await those who stray from the right path. However, the Tokoloshe is not merely a figure of fear; it also reflects deeper cultural themes, such as the struggle between order and chaos and the unseen forces that influence our lives. Traditional healers, known as sangomas, are crucial in addressing Tokoloshe disturbances. Through rituals and spiritual practices, they seek to cleanse spaces and protect individuals from the creature's influence. Tokoloshe's presence in modern folklore continues to captivate, its story adapted and retold in various forms, from literature to film, each iteration adding new layers to its mythos.

Communities have developed various practices to guard against Tokoloshe or to interact safely with it. One such technique involves making the Tokoloshe visible, often by enlisting the help of a sangoma to perform specific rituals or use special herbs. These practices aim to reveal the creature, stripping away its cloak of invisibility. Offerings might be made to ward off or appease Tokoloshe, or protective charms could be placed around the home. Such rituals serve not only to protect but also to acknowledge Tokoloshe's place in the spiritual landscape. Using raised beds is another common precaution, a practical measure to avoid nighttime disturbances attributed to this mischievous spirit. By elevating their sleeping quarters, individuals aim to place themselves out of reach, a simple yet effective strategy to ensure a peaceful night's rest.

Have you ever experienced something that seemed inexplicable, a moment where the ordinary shifted into the uncanny? Perhaps it was a misplaced object or a fleeting shadow in the corner of your eye. Take a moment to reflect on these experiences. Consider writing about them, exploring the emotions and thoughts they stirred. How do these moments connect with the stories you've heard or the cultural beliefs you hold? Use this space to delve into the personal and the mystical, finding meaning in the mysteries of life.

MAMI WATA: WATER SPIRITS ACROSS WEST AND CENTRAL AFRICA

Imagine standing by the edge of a vast, shimmering body of water. The horizon blurs where the water meets the sky, and in that magical space, Mami Wata reigns supreme. This powerful water spirit is celebrated across West and Central Africa, embodying the mysteries and beauty of the oceans, rivers, and lakes. Mami Wata is often depicted as an enchanting figure, sometimes as a mermaid with a fishtail and other times as a stunning woman draped in jewels and vibrant colors. Her allure is undeniable, capturing the imagination with her blend of elegance and power. But beneath her beauty lies a force that commands respect. Mami Wata is associated with wealth and fertility; her presence is a harbinger of prosperity and abundance. She is also a symbol of seduction, capable of drawing hearts with her captivating charm.

The legends of Mami Wata are as fluid and enchanting as the waters she embodies. One popular story tells of fishermen who, while casting their nets under the moonlit sky, encounter Mami Wata rising from the depths. Her appearance is both a blessing and a test, for she holds the power to bring fortune or misfortune. Those who show her respect and offer gifts of gratitude often find their nets overflowing with fish, a reward for their reverence. Yet, Mami Wata's interactions with humans are not purely transactional. Tales abound of her granting wealth and prosperity to those she favors, bestowing riches upon those who honor her with sincerity. But her relationships are not without complexity. Myths speak of romantic entanglements with humans, where Mami Wata's love becomes both a blessing and a curse, transforming lives with her touch.

Mami Wata holds a profound place in the cultural fabric of the regions she graces. Her image symbolizes beauty and power, revered and celebrated in countless communities. In local religious practices, Mami Wata is invoked as a deity who transcends the ordinary, bridging the gap between the human and the divine. Her influence extends beyond the spiritual, permeating the arts and literature of Africa. Artists capture her essence through vivid colors and flowing forms, while writers weave her tales into narratives that explore themes of identity, love, and transformation. Mami Wata's presence in modern African art and literature speaks to her enduring impact, a testament to her timeless allure and the cultural significance she holds.

Rituals dedicated to Mami Wata are elaborate and deeply spiritual, reflecting the reverence she commands. Offerings of perfume, jewelry, and sweet foods are common, each item chosen for its symbolic connection to Mami Wata's domains. Perfume, with its intoxicating scent, signifies allure and attraction, while jewelry represents wealth and status. Sweet foods are offerings of gratitude, a token of appreciation for her blessings. Priests and priestesses play a vital role in these ceremonies, guiding the community in acts of devotion and ensuring that the rituals are conducted with respect and sincerity. Annual festivals celebrating Mami Wata draw people together in joyous homage, where music, dance, and storytelling create a vibrant tapestry of worship and celebration.

Through these practices, Mami Wata's legacy is kept alive, her spirit an enduring presence in the hearts and minds of those who honor her. She is more than a myth; she is a living symbol of the power and mystery of the natural world, a reminder of the beauty and complexity that lies beneath the surface. Her stories invite us to explore the depths of our own experiences, find meaning in the ebb and flow of life, and celebrate the connections that bind us to each other and the world around us. Mami Wata's tale is one of transformation and transcendence, a journey through the waters of the soul where the line between the divine and the mundane blurs into a single, shimmering horizon.

THE GROOTSLANG: THE GREAT SERPENT OF SOUTHERN AFRICAN MYTH

Deep within the rugged terrain of Southern Africa, nestled among the rocky outcrops and hidden caves, lies a creature of myth and legend—the Grootslang. With its fearsome fangs and cunning nature, this colossal serpent is a sight to behold. Imagine a serpent so immense that its body stretches across the landscape, its scales shimmering like jewels in the sunlight. Some stories even attribute elephant-like features to this beast, suggesting a hybrid of unimaginable strength and mystery. The Grootslang is not merely a creature of brute force but a being of immense cunning, navigating the shadows and depths with ease. Its presence is both a warning and a challenge, a reminder of the power that lies beyond the familiar.

The tales of the Grootslang are rich with adventure and danger. One of the most famous legends tells of a hidden cave, known as the "Wonder Hole," said to be filled with diamonds. The Grootslang, as the eternal guardian of this treasure, ensures that only the bravest and most cunning adventurers dare approach. Many have tried their luck, hoping to outwit the serpent and claim the riches for themselves. Yet, the Grootslang's cunning is unmatched, and its strength is formidable, making it a challenge few can overcome. Some stories speak of adventurers who, through sheer wit and bravery, manage to escape the creature's wrath, while others tell of those who fall victim to its lethal embrace, their greed sealing their fate. The origins of the Grootslang are steeped in myth, with tales suggesting it was one of the first creatures created by the gods, who gave it both the strength of an elephant and the cunning of a serpent. When they realized their mistake, they split the creature into two, creating elephants and snakes. Yet, one Grootslang escaped and has roamed the earth ever since, guarding its treasures and evading capture.

In Southern African folklore, the Grootslang symbolizes both danger and wealth. Its presence in stories serves as a reminder of the perils that await those driven by greed and ambition. Yet, it also embodies the allure of untold riches, the promise of fortune that lies just beyond reach. The Grootslang's influence extends beyond oral traditions, finding its place in modern Southern African literature and media. From novels to films, its legend captivates audiences, offering a glimpse into the mysteries of the natural world and the human spirit. The Grootslang's impact on storytelling is profound, providing a canvas for exploring themes of courage, greed, and the eternal struggle between man and nature.

Communities living near the Grootslang's supposed haunts have developed rituals and practices to protect themselves from its wrath. Techniques for avoiding encounters often involve respecting the creature's territory, acknowledging its power, and steering clear of its lair. With their deep understanding of local lore, traditional healers play a crucial role in addressing Grootslang sightings. Through rituals and offerings, they seek to appease the creature, ensuring that balance is maintained and the community remains safe. These practices are not just about protection but about acknowledging the Grootslang's place in the spiritual and cultural landscape, honoring the ancient bond between humanity and the natural world.

The Grootslang's legend endures, a testament to the power of myth and the enduring allure of the unknown. Its story invites us to reflect on our own desires and fears, to consider the balance between ambition and caution. In the shadow of the Grootslang, we are reminded of the mysteries that lie beyond, waiting to be explored, understood, and respected. As you ponder the tales of this great serpent, let your imagination wander and find the threads of your own story woven into the mythic tapestry of the Grootslang.

ADZE: THE VAMPIRE SPIRITS OF THE EWE PEOPLE

In the quiet villages of Togo and Ghana, where the night air carries whispers of ancient tales, the Adze lurks as a creature of shadow and intrigue. This vampiric spirit, deeply rooted in Ewe folklore, possesses the unsettling ability to transform into a firefly or other small insect. Imagine a tiny creature slipping through the cracks of your home, undetected and unseen. In this form, the Adze is notorious for its sinister acts, known to suck blood and spread illness among unsuspecting villagers. Its presence is often associated with witchcraft and malevolent magic, casting a long shadow of fear and suspicion over the communities it haunts. The Adze embodies the darker side of the supernatural, a reminder of the unseen threats that hover just beyond the edge of the ordinary.

The myths surrounding the Adze are as chilling as they are captivating, weaving tales of blood and mystery that have been passed down through generations. One such story tells of a village plagued by mysterious illnesses, where livestock and people alike fell victim to an unseen predator. Villagers spoke of a firefly that seemed to linger near the afflicted, its presence coinciding with the onset of sickness. It wasn't long before the community came to suspect the work of the Adze, a creature said to prey on the weak and vulnerable under the cover of darkness. In another tale, a group of villagers managed to capture the Adze, trapping it in its firefly form. When confronted, the creature revealed its human guise, a shocking transformation that underscored Adze's connection to humanity and its potential to walk among us unnoticed. These stories delve into the origins of the Adze, offering explanations for its powers and its ties to the human world. Some myths suggest that the Adze was once a person cursed for their misdeeds, condemned to wander as a vampire spirit. Others speak of the Adze as a manifestation of dark magic, a being born from the shadows of human desire and ambition.

Within Ewe culture, the Adze holds a significant place as a symbol of fear and malevolence. Its story serves as a cautionary tale, reflecting the community's concerns about the dangers of the unknown and the power of malevolent forces. The Adze is woven into the fabric of local folklore, its presence a constant reminder of the thin line between the natural and the supernatural. In storytelling, the Adze often appears as a figure of dread, a creature to be avoided and respected. Its influence extends into modern Ewe literature and media, where it is portrayed as a symbol of the unseen threats that lurk within society. Through these narratives, the Adze continues to capture the imagination, offering a lens through which to explore themes of fear, power, and the human condition.

Communities have developed various methods to protect themselves from the Adze and to combat its influence. Identifying the Adze often involves looking for signs of its presence, such as unexplained illnesses and sightings of unusual insects. Once suspected, villagers may attempt to capture the creature in its firefly form, using nets or traps to contain it. Rituals to ward off the Adze are common, involving protective charms and objects designed to repel malevolent spirits. Traditional healers often lead these rituals and play a crucial role in safeguarding the community from supernatural threats. Through their knowledge of herbs and incantations, healers seek to cleanse spaces and protect individuals from Adze's influence. In some cases, offerings may be made to appease the creature, a gesture of respect and acknowledgment of its power. These practices are not just about protection but about maintaining balance and harmony, ensuring that the line between humans and the supernatural remains intact.

As we conclude this chapter, the world of mythological creatures opens a window into the rich tapestry of African folklore. Each entity, from the mischievous Tokoloshe to the enigmatic Adze, reflects the beliefs, fears, and hopes of the communities that tell their stories. These myths invite us to explore the unseen forces that shape our world, offering a glimpse into the mysteries that lie just beneath the surface. As we move forward, we will delve into the fables and moral stories that have guided generations, exploring the lessons they impart and the values they uphold.

CHAPTER 10: FABLES AND MORAL STORIES

U nder the canopy of the African night, the fire crackles and dances, casting shadows that flicker like old memories. Here, on the red earth of a West African village, stories find their voice. Imagine the air thick with anticipation as the storyteller, the griot, begins to weave a tale. It is the tale of Anansi the Spider, a figure who has long spun his web across the imagination of the people. With his cunning and charm, Anansi is not just a character but a force, a symbol of the cleverness and wit that thread through the rich tapestry of African folklore.

Anansi originates from Akan mythology, where he is more than a simple trickster; he is the embodiment of storytelling itself. The name Anansi comes from the Akan word for "spider," which is fitting. Like a spider weaving its web, Anansi crafts his stories with intricate care, each strand connecting to the next. His tales traveled with the Ashanti people from Ghana across the Atlantic, carried in the hearts and minds of those enduring the hardships of slavery. In the Caribbean, Anansi became a cultural hero, a figure of resistance and survival, his stories serving as a means of escape and education.

One of the most cherished tales is "Anansi and the Pot of Wisdom." In this story, Anansi attempts to gather all the world's wisdom into a clay pot, intending to hoard it for himself. He plans to hide it high in a tree, away from those who might seek its treasures. But as he struggles to climb, the pot tied awkwardly to his front, his young son suggests it would be easier to carry it on his back. Anansi realizes he doesn't possess all the wisdom; even a child sees what he does not. The pot slips and shatters, scattering wisdom across the earth. This story reminds us of the folly of greed and the importance of sharing knowledge.

Then there's "Anansi and the Turtle," a tale about hospitality and fairness. One day, Anansi invites Turtle to dinner but tricks him by providing food only when Turtle's hands are too dirty to eat. In retaliation, Turtle later invites Anansi to a meal underwater, knowing Anansi cannot hold his breath. The story cleverly teaches that fairness and reciprocity are cornerstones of community life, emphasizing that what goes around truly comes around.

In "Anansi and the Sky God," Anansi seeks to own all the stories of the world, which are in the possession of Nyame, the Sky God. To win them, Anansi must capture three formidable creatures: a python, a leopard, and a hornet. Through clever tricks and cunning plans, he succeeds, earning the right to be the keeper of stories. This tale highlights the value of storytelling and the cleverness needed to overcome seemingly insurmountable challenges.

Anansi's stories resonate deeply, reflecting the societal norms and values of the communities that tell them. Anansi embodies wit and resourcefulness, traits that have been celebrated and admired across cultures. His tales are not merely entertainment; they are lessons wrapped in humor and wit, teaching children about the complexities of human behavior. In many ways, Anansi is a mirror, reflecting both the light and shadow within us all.

In modern times, Anansi's influence continues to thrive. His stories are woven into the fabric of Caribbean and African-American folklore, a testament to their enduring appeal. Anansi appears in literature, comics, and television, his character adapting to new contexts while retaining his core essence. Whether through the pages of a book or the screen of a television, Anansi's tales continue to captivate and educate, bridging the past and present in a way that only a master storyteller can. His web stretches far and wide, connecting generations and cultures with the timeless threads of wisdom and wit.

THE TORTOISE AND THE LEOPARD: A TALE OF WIT AND CUNNING

Picture the vast African savannah, where the golden grass sways under the sun's embrace and the horizon seems endless. Here, amidst the whisper of the wind and the rustle of leaves, lives a cast of characters whose stories have been told for generations. Among them is the tortoise, a creature known not for speed or strength but for its cleverness and cunning. With its hard shell and slow gait, it seems an unlikely hero. Yet, within its modest exterior lies a sharp mind, always ready to devise a plan.

In contrast, stands the leopard, a predator whose strength and agility make it a feared presence among the savannah's dwellers. With sleek fur and silent paws, the leopard's prowess is unmatched, its hunger a force to be reckoned with. The savannah itself, a landscape of beauty and danger, serves as the backdrop for their encounters, where wit and strength come to a head.

In one of the most cherished tales, the leopard sets a trap for the tortoise, eager to make a meal of the slow-moving creature. The tortoise, however, is not so easily caught. Seeing the trap, the tortoise pretends to stumble into it, allowing the leopard to think it has won. As the leopard approaches, confident in its victory, the tortoise begins to sing a song, its voice soft and steady. The song, filled with clever words and hidden meanings, distracts the leopard just long enough for the tortoise to wriggle free. In that moment, the tortoise's wit outshines the leopard's strength, turning the hunter into the fool. The leopard, bewildered and frustrated, learns that brawn alone cannot conquer a sharp mind.

The moral lesson of this tale is clear: intelligence can triumph over brute strength. Through the tortoise's actions, we see the power of strategic thinking and problem-solving. In African societies, stories like this one emphasize the value of wit and intelligence, traits that are celebrated as much as, if not more than, physical strength. These fables teach that true power lies not in the muscles but in the mind. The tortoise's ability to outsmart the leopard serves as a reminder that even the most formidable challenges can be overcome with careful thought and cunning. It's a lesson that resonates across cultures and generations, encouraging listeners to look beyond appearances and to value the power of cleverness and strategic planning.

Variations of the tortoise and leopard tale exist across different African regions, each adding its own unique flavor to the story. In some versions, the tortoise is replaced by a hare or a bird, yet the core message remains the same. These adaptations highlight the universal appeal of the story and the shared values it conveys. In certain cultures, the leopard may be depicted as more sympathetic, acting out of necessity rather than malice. This nuance adds depth to the fable, encouraging empathy and understanding.

The differences in character portrayal and moral emphasis reflect the diverse cultural landscapes of Africa, where stories adapt to the needs and values of their tellers. Whether told in a village under the stars or shared in a bustling city, the tale of the tortoise and the leopard continues to captivate and inspire, its wisdom timeless and enduring.

As you reflect on this story, consider its relevance to your own life. Have there been moments when wit and cunning have helped you overcome a challenge? Perhaps there's a situation where the strength of your mind has proven more valuable than physical might. The tortoise and leopard remind us that there is always more than one way to navigate the world, and sometimes, the most unassuming path leads to the greatest victory. In the dance between predator and prey, the unexpected often holds the most power.

THE LION'S WHISKER: A STORY OF PATIENCE AND PERSEVERANCE

In a village nestled between rolling hills and verdant fields, life unfolds with a rhythm as ancient as the land itself. People go about their daily routines, tending to crops and livestock, exchanging stories by the fireside. Among them lives a wise healer, a figure of respect and reverence, known for her knowledge of herbs and the mysteries of the spirit world. One day, a woman approaches the healer, her face etched with worry and hope. She seeks a potion to mend a fractured relationship with her stepson, a boy whose trust she yearns to earn. After a moment's thought, the healer listens and tells her that to complete the potion. She must bring back a whisker from a lion—a task as daunting as it is dangerous. The lion, a creature of regal power and fierce independence, roams the nearby savannah, a symbol of both challenge and danger.

Determined to achieve her goal, the woman sets out each day to the edge of the savannah, where the lion is known to rest. She does not approach hastily but instead, takes her time, observing the lion from a distance. With each sunrise, she moves a little closer, careful not to alarm the great beast. She offers it food, leaving it at the edge of its territory, and sits quietly, allowing the lion to grow accustomed to her presence. Over weeks, a bond of trust begins to form. The lion, no longer viewing her as a threat, allows her nearer. Her patience and perseverance become her allies, guiding her through this delicate dance of trust and respect. Finally, one day, she finds herself close enough to gently pluck a whisker from the lion's mane. She returns to the healer, her heart full of gratitude and awe for what she has accomplished.

The fable of the lion's whisker carries profound cultural significance, touching upon themes that resonate deeply within us. It speaks to the power of patience and determination, illustrating how, through steady effort and resolve, even the most formidable challenges can be overcome. The woman's journey is a testament to the virtues of careful planning and building trust—lessons that hold true whether dealing with wild creatures or navigating life's interpersonal relationships. Her success is not just in acquiring the whisker but in the transformation she undergoes, learning that change often requires time and a gentle approach. In African societies, these values are celebrated and passed down, teaching that perseverance is not about force but about the quiet strength that lies in persistence.

In modern cultural practices, the story of the lion's whisker continues to impart wisdom and guidance. It is a tale often shared with children, illustrating that patience and perseverance are crucial in achieving their dreams. As a moral lesson, it encourages them to approach challenges with a calm mind and a steady heart, underscoring the idea that quick solutions are not always the best ones. The fable's themes find their way into literature and media, adapted into stories and films exploring the dynamics of human relationships and the importance of understanding and empathy. Whether through a book or a classroom lesson, the lion's whisker remains a powerful metaphor for the journey towards trust and reconciliation, a reminder of the enduring power of patience.

The story also invites reflection on how these themes play out in our lives. In relationships, whether personal or professional, the ability to listen, to wait, and to build trust is invaluable. The woman's quest for the lion's whisker is not just about the physical task but about the transformation within, a metamorphosis that speaks to the heart of human experience. Through her patience, she learns to see the world through the lion's eyes, an understanding that transcends fear and fosters connection. As you think about this tale, consider where patience and perseverance have guided you and where they have led you to places you might not have reached otherwise.

THE THREE BROTHERS AND THE POT OF WISDOM: A LESSON IN HUMILITY

In a small village nestled among rolling hills, where the sun painted the skies with warm hues every morning, lived three brothers, each unique in their disposition. The eldest brother was known for his pride, always walking with his head held high, thinking himself superior to others. His confidence often bordered on arrogance, blinding him to the wisdom of those around him. The middle brother, driven by ambition, sought power and recognition. His dreams were grand, but his impatience often led him astray. Then there was the youngest brother, humble and observant, always willing to listen and learn. He valued kindness and had a quiet strength that drew people to him.

In the heart of their village resided a wise elder who possessed a pot of wisdom. This pot was said to contain the knowledge of the ages, a treasure that many desired but few could handle. Hearing tales of the pot's power, the brothers decided to seek it out, each with their own motives. The journey was fraught with challenges, as they navigated dense forests, crossed treacherous rivers, and faced the biting cold of the mountain peaks. This odyssey revealed their true characters.

The eldest brother, driven by pride, rushed ahead, dismissing the advice of those they met. He believed his strength and status would see him through. But in his haste, he stumbled, falling prey to the traps of the forest, his pride blinding him to danger. The middle brother, eager to prove himself, pushed forward with determination. He sought shortcuts, thinking he could outsmart the journey itself. Yet, his impatience led him to falter, as he missed crucial signs and paths that would have guided him safely.

The youngest brother, however, approached the journey with humility. He listened to the whispers of the wind and the stories of the trees, learning from the land itself. He took his time, observing the world around him, and in doing so, gained insights that his brothers had overlooked. When he finally reached the wise elder, his humility and willingness to learn earned him the pot of wisdom. He understood that true wisdom came not from the pot but from the journey and the lessons learned along the way.

This fable holds deep cultural significance, emphasizing humility and respect for knowledge. It teaches us that character, not birthright, defines our path. In many African societies, wisdom is revered above all else, and this story reminds us that it is not given lightly. The youngest brother's success underscores the importance of approaching life with an open heart and mind, valuing learning over arrogance.

Across Africa, variations of this story echo the same themes, each adapted to fit the cultural context of its tellers. In some versions, sisters might replace the brothers, or the pot of wisdom might take the form of a magical tree or a sacred river. These adaptations highlight the story's universal appeal as well as its adaptability to different cultures and values. While the characters and settings may change, the core message remains: humility and a willingness to learn are the true paths to wisdom.

As we close this chapter, we've journeyed through stories that teach and inspire, each with its own unique lessons. From Anansi's cunning to the patience of the woman seeking the lion's whisker, these tales reflect the rich cultural heritage of Africa, offering wisdom and insight that resonate across time and space. Next, we will explore the deities and historical icons that have shaped the spiritual and cultural landscape of the continent. Like the stories we've shared, these figures hold lessons and legacies that continue to influence and inspire.

CHAPTER 11: DETAILED EXPLORATION OF SPECIFIC DEITIES AND DEIFIED HISTORICAL ICONS

Africa's deities and deified historical icons embody the values, struggles, and triumphs of the communities that revere them. These figures are not only worshipped as gods but also serve as powerful symbols of the human experience, reflecting themes of creation, transformation, protection, and nurturing. This chapter explores two prominent deities from Yoruba mythology—Ogun, the god of iron and war, and Yemoja, the mother of all Orishas—as well as two iconic historical figures: Nzinga Mbande, the queen of Ndongo and Matamba, and Haile Selassie, the Emperor of Ethiopia. Through their stories and worship, we gain insight into the cultural and spiritual significance of these figures and their enduring influence on African society.

Ogun, the god of iron and war, is a powerful figure in Yoruba mythology, embodying both the creative and destructive forces of iron. He is revered as a craftsman, a warrior, and a protector, whose influence stretches from the anvils of blacksmiths to the heat of battlefields. Ogun's mastery of metallurgy is central to his identity, with iron representing strength, transformation, and resilience. His tools—the anvil, hammer, and machete—are symbols of his power, reflecting his role in shaping the world through both creation and destruction. As a warrior deity, Ogun is also a guardian of truth and justice, inspiring courage in those who stand against oppression.

Yemoja, the mother of all Orishas, embodies the nurturing spirit of water, representing both the life-giving and protective forces of nature. Her domain includes rivers and oceans, and she is revered as the goddess of fertility and motherhood. Yemoja's influence extends to childbirth, where she is called upon to ensure the safety of mothers and their newborns. One enduring myth tells of Yemoja's tears creating rivers and oceans, symbolizing her deep connection to water as a source of life and renewal. Her nurturing presence is evident in her role as the protector and guide of her children, the Orishas, ensuring that they fulfill their divine purposes and maintain harmony.

Nzinga Mbande, the formidable queen of Ndongo and Matamba, was not just a ruler; she was a symbol of resistance and resilience. In the early 17th century, when Portuguese colonizers sought to expand their territories and control the slave trade, Nzinga rose to meet this threat with diplomacy and military prowess. She used her wit to navigate the complex political landscape, forging strategic alliances, including with the Dutch, to resist colonial encroachment. One famous event was her negotiation with the Portuguese, where she commanded an attendant to serve as a makeshift throne, asserting her equality and demonstrating her strength of character. Nzinga's legacy is immortalized in symbols like the spear and shield, emblematic of her role as a defender. Her story continues to inspire, offering a narrative of strength and determination.

Haile Selassie, the Emperor of Ethiopia, was a visionary leader whose legacy stretches far beyond his homeland. His reign marked a period of transformation, as he sought to modernize Ethiopia through reforms in education, infrastructure, and legal systems. Selassie's leadership during the Italian invasion further cemented his status as a symbol of defiance against imperialism. His powerful speech at the League of Nations emphasized justice and collective security, warning of the dangers of unchecked aggression. Selassie also played a pivotal role in founding the Organization of African Unity (OAU), promoting African unity and independence. He is revered within Rastafarian beliefs as a divine figure embodying liberation, equality, and spiritual awakening. His influence is felt in global Pan-Africanism and liberation movements, serving as a symbol of defiance against oppression and a belief in collective action.

Ogun, Yemoja, Nzinga Mbande, and Haile Selassie are just a few of the many deities and deified historical icons that play significant roles in African spirituality and history.

Their stories and legacies offer profound insights into the values and beliefs of the communities that venerate them. Ogun's strength and resilience, Yemoja's nurturing nature, Nzinga's defiance, and Selassie's vision reflect the dualities inherent in the human experience—creation and destruction, courage and compassion, strength and perseverance. By exploring these figures, we gain a deeper understanding of the cultural and spiritual heritage of Africa and the enduring connection between the divine, the historical, and the human.

OGUN: THE GOD OF IRON AND WAR

Have you ever listened to the sound of a blacksmith's hammer ringing out in the early morning, each strike a heartbeat of creation and transformation? This is the resonance of Ogun, the god of iron and war in Yoruba mythology, echoing through the ages. Imagine a figure who embodies both the creative and destructive forces of iron. Ogun stands at the crossroads of these energies, wielding power and wisdom in equal measure. His domain stretches from the anvils of blacksmiths to the heat of battlefields, where his influence shapes the world. As a deity, Ogun is much more than a warrior; he is a craftsman, a protector, and a symbol of transformation. His story is woven into the very fabric of Yoruba culture, reflecting the duality of creation and destruction inherent in human experience.

Ogun's association with iron is central to his identity and power. In Yoruba mythology, iron is not just a metal; it is a living force, a symbol of strength, transformation, and resilience. Ogun is revered for his mastery of metallurgy, his ability to shape raw materials into tools and weapons that serve both creation and destruction. The anvil, the hammer, and the machete are more than mere objects; they are extensions of Ogun's will, symbols of his dominion over the elements. His prowess in metalwork is celebrated in myths that speak of his role as a blacksmith, a craftsman who cleared paths for the Orishas with his iron tools, opening the way for civilization to flourish. Ogun's connection to iron extends beyond the physical; it speaks to the transformative power of labor and perseverance, the ability to mold one's destiny through hard work and determination.

Ogun's role as a warrior deity is equally significant, embodying the fierce spirit of a protector. In the Yoruba pantheon, Ogun is a guardian of truth and justice, a deity who fights for righteousness and order. His presence in battle is a source of strength and courage, inspiring those who stand against oppression and chaos. The myths of Ogun's battles and victories are tales of valor and strategy, narratives that celebrate his prowess as a warrior and leader. One such story recounts how Ogun led the Orishas to victory in a great war, using his iron tools to clear a path through the dense forest, enabling his allies to advance and triumph. This myth underscores Ogun's strategic brilliance and unwavering commitment to his people. His legacy as a warrior is not confined to the battlefield; it extends to the realms of social justice and protection, where his influence guides those who seek to uphold truth and integrity.

In Yoruba art and iconography, Ogun is depicted with symbols that reflect his multifaceted nature. The iron tools and weapons are prominent representations of his power, capturing the essence of his dual role as creator and destroyer. The color green is also associated with Ogun, symbolizing fertility, growth, and renewal. This color speaks to the cyclical nature of life and the transformative power of the earth, elements that are intrinsic to Ogun's identity. In rituals and religious practices, Ogun is venerated through offerings that honor his connection to iron and labor. Common offerings include iron objects, palm wine, and red meat, each symbolizing strength, transformation, and sacrifice. These offerings are made at sacred sites, where devotees gather to seek Ogun's blessing and guidance. The role of blacksmiths and warriors in Ogun's worship is vital, as they embody the values of hard work, resilience, and courage that define his legacy.

Annual festivals and ceremonies dedicated to Ogun are vibrant expressions of faith and community. During these events, music, dance, and storytelling come together to celebrate Ogun's contributions to society. Participants engage in rituals that invoke Ogun's presence, seeking his protection and favor. These festivals are more than religious observances; they are communal gatherings that reinforce the bonds between individuals and their shared cultural heritage. Through these practices, Ogun's spirit is kept alive, his influence enduring in the hearts and minds of those who honor him. In the stories of Ogun, we find reflections of our own struggles and triumphs, reminders of the power and potential that lie within each of us to shape our destinies and embrace the divine.

YEMOJA: THE MOTHER OF ALL ORISHAS

Picture standing by a river at dawn, the air cool and filled with the sound of flowing water. This is where the essence of Yemoja, the mother of all Orishas, comes alive. Yemoja embodies the nurturing spirit of water, representing both the life-giving and protective forces of nature. Her domain includes rivers and oceans, the vast bodies of water that sustain life. In Yoruba mythology, Yemoja is revered as the goddess of fertility and motherhood, a presence that comforts and guides. Her influence extends to childbirth, where she is called upon to ensure the safety of mothers and their newborns. Her name is whispered in prayers, a call for her gentle strength and wisdom to watch over families and communities. Her nurturing presence is not just seen in the physical world but felt in the spiritual connections she fosters among her followers.

One of the most enduring myths about Yemoja is the tale of her tears creating rivers and oceans. According to the story, when Yemoja wept, her tears flowed and transformed into the rivers and seas that nourish the earth. This myth speaks to her deep connection with water as a source of life and renewal. Her tears are not just a symbol of sorrow but of hope and regeneration, a reminder that life continues through cycles of growth and change. Yemoja is also known for her role in guiding and protecting her children, the Orishas. As their mother, she offers wisdom and care, ensuring that they fulfill their divine purposes. Her influence is evident in the way she encourages harmony and balance among the Orishas, reflecting her desire for unity and peace. In the creation of the first humans, Yemoja's nurturing spirit is again at the forefront, as she blesses humanity with the gifts of life and love.

In Yoruba art and iconography, Yemoja is depicted in ways that highlight her connection to water and fertility. The river and sea shells are powerful symbols of her domain, representing her role as the guardian of the waters. These elements are often used in artistic depictions to convey her grace and strength, capturing the essence of her divine presence. The color blue, associated with Yemoja, symbolizes the depths of the ocean and the tranquility of water, reflecting her calming influence. This color is prevalent in the garments and adornments used in her worship, creating a visual connection to her aquatic realm. Through these symbols, Yemoja's representation in Yoruba culture is both profound and revered, celebrating her as a source of life and protection.

Rituals and practices dedicated to Yemoja are integral to Yoruba religious life, offering a way for devotees to honor and connect with her. Common offerings to Yemoja include fish, water, and white cloth, each symbolizing aspects of her domain and influence. These offerings are made at sacred sites, such as rivers or ocean shores, where her presence is believed to be strongest. Women, especially mothers, play a significant role in Yemoja's worship, reflecting her connection to fertility and motherhood. They lead prayers and rituals, seeking Yemoja's guidance and protection for their families. Annual festivals and ceremonies held in her honor are vibrant celebrations of her contributions to the community. Participants gather by the water, adorned in blue and white, singing songs of praise and gratitude. These gatherings are not just religious observances but communal events that strengthen bonds and foster a sense of unity. Through these practices, Yemoja's spirit is celebrated and her influence felt in the lives of those who call upon her.

NZINGA MBANDE: THE WARRIOR QUEEN AND HER DEIFICATION

Imagine the vibrant lands of Central Africa, where legends tell of a queen who stood unyielding against the tides of colonial power. Nzinga Mbande, the formidable queen of Ndongo and Matamba, was not just a ruler; she was a symbol of resistance and resilience. Her story begins in the early 17th century, a time when Portuguese colonizers sought to expand their territories and control the lucrative slave trade. Nzinga, with a keen mind and unyielding spirit, rose to meet this threat with diplomacy and military prowess. She was a leader who understood the art of negotiation, using her wit and intelligence to navigate the complex political landscape of her time. Her reign was marked by a fierce determination to protect her people and preserve their autonomy. Nzinga's legacy is one of defiance and strength, a testament to her role as both a warrior and a queen. Her ability to lead in times of crisis solidified her place as a revered figure in African history.

Nzinga's life is filled with moments that showcase her extraordinary leadership and resilience. One of the most famous events in her life was her negotiation with the Portuguese, which has become legendary for its display of dignity and assertiveness. During a meeting with the Portuguese governor, Nzinga arrived to find that no chair had been provided for her, a subtle attempt to demean her status. Undeterred, Nzinga commanded one of her attendants to kneel and serve as a makeshift throne. This act of defiance not only asserted her equality but also demonstrated her resourcefulness and strength of character. Her negotiations were not limited to diplomacy; Nzinga also forged strategic alliances to bolster her military campaigns. She allied with the Dutch, effectively leveraging their support to combat Portuguese forces. These alliances were crucial in her efforts to resist colonial encroachment and maintain control over her territories. Nzinga's ability to adapt and form meaningful partnerships speaks to her strategic brilliance and commitment to her people's freedom.

Nzinga is immortalized in the symbols that capture her warrior spirit and unyielding resolve. The spear and shield symbolize her role as a defender, representing her courage and readiness to fight for her people. In Angolan art and cultural expressions, Nzinga is often depicted as a powerful figure, embodying the strength and resilience of her people. Her image serves as a reminder of the resistance and empowerment she inspired in those around her. Nzinga's legacy extends beyond her military achievements; she is a symbol of empowerment and defiance against oppression. Her story resonates across generations, offering a narrative of strength and determination that continues to inspire. As a cultural icon, Nzinga represents the enduring spirit of resistance that defines African history, a testament to the power of leadership and the impact one individual can have on shaping the course of events.

Nzinga Mbande's deification and cultural impact are profound, as she is revered and remembered in modern culture as both a historical figure and a symbol of empowerment. In contemporary Angolan folklore, Nzinga is celebrated as a national hero, her story woven into the fabric of the country's cultural identity. Annual commemorations and celebrations honor her legacy, bringing people together to reflect on her contributions and the lessons her life imparts. Nzinga's influence extends beyond Angola, resonating with African and African diasporic feminist movements. Her story of defiance and leadership inspires those who seek to challenge societal norms and advocate for gender equality. Nzinga's legacy is a powerful reminder of the strength and resilience that lie within each of us, urging us to embrace our own potential for change and impact. Through her life and legacy, Nzinga Mbande continues to inspire and empower, a beacon of hope and resistance that shines brightly across time and space.

HAILE SELASSIE: THE LION OF JUDAH AND HIS MYTHIC STATUS

Imagine waking up in the bustling heart of Ethiopia during the early 20th century, where history and tradition intertwine with the aspirations of a nation on the cusp of change. This was the world of Haile Selassie, a ruler whose legacy stretches far beyond the borders of his homeland. As the Emperor of Ethiopia, Selassie's reign marked a period of transformation and resilience. He was a visionary leader who sought to modernize his nation, introducing reforms that touched every aspect of Ethiopian life. Education, infrastructure, and legal systems were just a few areas that witnessed his determination to propel Ethiopia into the modern era. His leadership during the Italian invasion further cemented his mythic status. Faced with aggression from Mussolini's forces, Selassie became a symbol of defiance, rallying his people and the world in a stand against imperialism. Even in exile, his spirit remained unbroken. He spoke boldly at the League of Nations, calling for international support and highlighting the dangers of unchecked aggression.

These moments capture the essence of Selassie's enduring influence. His appeal to the League of Nations was a defining event, not just for Ethiopia but for the global community. Standing before the assembly, Selassie delivered a powerful speech, emphasizing the principles of justice and collective security. He warned that the aggression faced by Ethiopia could spread if not addressed, a prescient insight that resonated deeply as World War II unfolded. After years of struggle, his return to Ethiopia in 1941 marked a triumphant restoration of his rule, supported by the efforts of Ethiopian patriots and Allied forces. This victory was not merely a personal triumph but a testament to the resilience of the Ethiopian people and their unwavering belief in sovereignty and justice.

Moreover, Selassie's vision extended beyond Ethiopia's borders. He played a pivotal role in the founding of the Organization of African Unity (OAU) in 1963, a landmark achievement that underscored his commitment to African unity and independence. The OAU became a powerful platform for promoting decolonization and fostering cooperation among African nations. Selassie's advocacy for African unity was rooted in his belief that the continent's strength lay in solidarity and collaboration. His leadership inspired generations of African leaders and movements, reinforcing the idea that unity was key to overcoming the challenges posed by colonial legacies and global inequities.

Throughout his life, Selassie was often referred to as the "Lion of Judah," a title steeped in symbolism and authority. This designation reflected his royal lineage, tracing back to the biblical King Solomon and the Queen of Sheba. The Lion of Judah became a powerful emblem of his reign, representing strength, courage, and legitimacy. In Ethiopian art and cultural expressions, Selassie's image is often intertwined with these symbols, capturing his role as a unifying figure and a beacon of hope for his people. He is depicted in regal attire, surrounded by motifs that celebrate his legacy and contributions to Ethiopia's cultural heritage.

Selassie's impact extends into the spiritual realm, where he holds a revered place in Rastafarian beliefs. Within this movement, he is considered a divine figure, embodying the values of liberation, equality, and spiritual awakening. Rastafarians view Selassie as a messianic figure, whose teachings and leadership offer guidance and inspiration. Annual celebrations and rituals honoring Selassie's legacy are integral to Rastafarian practice, reinforcing his influence as a symbol of resilience and empowerment. His philosophy of unity and justice resonates deeply within the Rastafarian community, where his teachings continue to inspire a commitment to social justice and cultural pride.

Beyond religious reverence, Selassie's influence is felt in global Pan-Africanism and liberation movements. His advocacy for African independence and unity contributed to a broader dialogue on racial equality and self-determination. Selassie's legacy serves as a touchstone for those who continue to fight for justice and equality, embodying a spirit of defiance against oppression and a steadfast belief in the power of collective action. Through his life and legacy, Haile Selassie remains a towering figure, a symbol of hope and strength that transcends borders and generations. His story is a reminder of the enduring impact of leadership and the transformative power of vision and courage.

CHAPTER 12: INFLUENCE OF ANCIENT MYTHS ON MODERN CULTURE

You're on a vibrant street in Havana, Cuba, where the intoxicating rhythm of drums fills the air, and people dance with a joyful abandon that seems to transcend time. As the sun sets, a procession emerges, colorful and alive, carrying with it the echoes of a world far across the Atlantic Ocean. This scene is not merely a spectacle; it is a living testament to the enduring legacy of Orisha worship, a tradition that has journeyed across continents and centuries to find a new home in the Americas. The worship of Orishas, the deities of the Yoruba people, was carried to the Americas through the transatlantic slave trade, a dark chapter in history that saw millions of Africans uprooted from their homelands. Yet, even in the face of unimaginable hardship, these enslaved individuals held onto their spiritual practices, adapting them to new environments and blending them with local beliefs.

The resilience of African slaves in preserving their spiritual practices is a testament to the power of faith and community. Despite the oppressive conditions they faced, they found ways to keep their traditions alive, often in secret, away from the watchful eyes of their oppressors. The organized and urbanized socio-religious structure of the Yoruba

Orisha, as detailed in scholarly articles, played a significant role in its transportability and reconstruction in the New World. This structure allowed Yoruba religious practices to eclipse those of other groups, becoming dominant in regions like Trinidad, Brazil, and Cuba. The blending of Orisha worship with Catholicism and other local beliefs gave rise to syncretic religions that are vibrant and unique.

In Cuba, the formation of Santería exemplifies this blend. Santería combines the worship of Yoruba Orishas with Catholic saints, creating a rich tapestry of faith that is both African and Cuban. Devotees celebrate through music and dance, connecting with the divine in ways that honor their ancestors while embracing new cultural elements. The rhythmic beats of the batá drums guide the dancers, their movements echoing the stories and spirits of the Orishas. This dance is a sacred act, a form of communication with the divine that transcends words. Santería festivals are lively and colorful, drawing people from all walks of life to partake in the celebration of faith and community.

In Brazil, Candomblé serves as another example of the fusion between African and local traditions. Here, Yoruba, Fon, and Bantu deities merge with Catholic elements, creating a religion that is as diverse as the country itself. The terreiros, or places of worship, are vibrant spaces where music, dance, and ritual come together to create a powerful spiritual experience. Candomblé ceremonies are elaborate and immersive, involving drumming, singing, and the invocation of Orishas through trance and possession. These ceremonies are not just religious events; they are cultural celebrations that reinforce the identity and unity of the community.

Haiti's Vodou also reflects the blending of Yoruba and Fon deities with Catholicism. Vodou is a religion that has often been misunderstood and misrepresented, yet it holds deep cultural significance for its practitioners. Vodou ceremonies are characterized by drumming, dancing, and the invocation of spirits known as lwa, who are akin to the Orishas. These ceremonies serve as a means of connecting with ancestors, seeking guidance, and healing. The vibrant colors of the altars, the smell of incense, and the sound of drums create an atmosphere that is both sacred and communal. Vodou, like Santería and Candomblé, is a religion that speaks to the resilience and adaptability of African spiritual traditions.

The cultural impact of these syncretic religions is profound, influencing the cultural landscape of their respective countries in numerous ways. Music and dance are integral to religious ceremonies, serving as a means of connecting with the divine and expressing devotion. The rhythms of the drums and the movements of the dancers are not just artistic expressions; they are acts of worship that embody the spirit of the Orishas. These religions have also influenced local festivals and celebrations, adding a rich layer of cultural diversity and heritage.

The representation of Orishas in visual arts and literature further illustrates their enduring influence. Artists and writers draw inspiration from the stories and symbols of Orisha worship, creating works that celebrate the beauty and complexity of these traditions. In literature, the Orishas come to life as characters, their stories woven into narratives that explore themes of identity, resilience, and spirituality. In visual arts, the vibrant colors and intricate designs of Orisha-inspired works capture the imagination and evoke a sense of wonder.

In recent years, there has been a modern revival and global spread of Orisha worship, with the African diaspora playing a key role in promoting these traditions. Communities dedicated to Orisha worship have emerged in North America and Europe, providing spaces for people to connect with their spiritual heritage. These communities are vibrant and diverse, welcoming individuals of all backgrounds who seek to explore and embrace the wisdom of Orisha worship.

The influence of popular culture and media has also contributed to the global perception of Orisha worship. Films, music, and literature have introduced these traditions to a wider audience, sparking interest and curiosity. The portrayal of Orishas in media often highlights their power and beauty, inviting viewers to explore the rich tapestry of African spirituality. This global recognition has led to a renewed appreciation for the cultural and spiritual contributions of Orisha worship, fostering a sense of pride and connection among those who embrace these traditions.

To further engage with the rich history and cultural impact of Orisha worship, consider the following reflection exercise. Think about how these traditions have shaped your understanding of identity and spirituality. How do they resonate with your own experiences and beliefs? Take a moment to reflect on the connections you feel to these stories and practices. You might even explore how music and dance have influenced your life, drawing parallels between personal experiences and the cultural expressions found in Santería, Candomblé, and Vodou.

As you continue exploring the legacy of Orisha worship, remember that these traditions are not just relics of the past; they are living, evolving expressions of faith and identity. They offer a unique perspective on the interconnectedness of cultures and the enduring power of spirituality to transcend time and space. Whether through the vibrant rhythms of a Santería drumming session, the intricate dance of a Candomblé ceremony, or the deep spiritual connection felt in a Vodou ritual, Orisha worship continues to inspire and transform lives across the globe.

AFROFUTURISM: REIMAGINING AFRICAN MYTHOLOGY IN MODERN MEDIA

Afrofuturism is a cultural movement that boldly reimagines African culture and mythology through the lens of futuristic contexts. This genre is where African heritage meets the boundless possibilities of tomorrow, where ancient myths blend seamlessly with the cutting-edge realms of technology and speculative fiction. At its core, Afrofuturism is about resilience and identity, drawing strength from the past while envisioning a future filled with hope and innovation. It allows African narratives to transcend time, offering a space where cultural heritage is not only preserved but celebrated. This movement challenges traditional narratives, painting a world where African people are not just participants but leaders in shaping the future. The fusion of African mythology with modern technology creates a rich tapestry that is both familiar and fantastical. It invites readers and viewers alike to engage with stories deeply rooted in tradition, yet unafraid to explore new frontiers.

In literature, Afrofuturism has found a strong voice through authors who weave African myths into the fabric of their speculative fiction works. Octavia Butler, often regarded as a pioneer of the genre, infused her novels with themes inspired by African folklore. Her works explore complex ideas about race, gender, and power, all while drawing from a rich mythological backdrop. In "Kindred," Butler time-travels her characters to confront the harsh realities of slavery, intertwining these experiences with the timeless resilience found in African myths. Similarly, Nnedi Okorafor brings Nigerian mythology to life in her novels "Binti" and "Akata Witch," where she crafts worlds rich with tradition and magic. Okorafor's characters navigate these worlds with a grace that reflects their cultural heritage, blending mythological elements with futuristic settings. Her stories celebrate African identity, offering readers a glimpse into a world where the past and future coexist harmoniously. In his novel "Rosewater," Tade Thompson delves into Yoruba cosmology, creating a narrative that is both thrilling and thought-provoking. Thompson's exploration of Yoruba beliefs is woven into a science fiction narrative that challenges perceptions of reality and identity. Through these literary works, Afrofuturism provides a platform for African mythology to flourish, inspiring readers to appreciate the depth and complexity of these timeless stories.

Visual arts and media also play a significant role in the Afrofuturist movement, depicting African mythology through innovative and compelling lenses. The film "Black Panther" serves as a prime example of how Afrofuturism can captivate global audiences. Set in the fictional African nation of Wakanda, the movie portrays a technologically advanced society that draws heavily from African cultural motifs. The visual aesthetics of Wakanda are a celebration of African heritage, showcasing traditional attire and architecture alongside futuristic technology. This fusion of the ancient and the modern creates a powerful narrative that resonates with viewers, offering a vision of Africa that is both aspirational and grounded in reality. Music videos and fashion have also embraced Afrofuturist themes, incorporating African-inspired motifs that celebrate cultural pride and innovation. Artists like Janelle Monáe use their platforms to challenge stereotypes, blending music, fashion, and visual art to create a unique Afrofuturist aesthetic. Monáe's work is a testament to the power of Afrofuturism to influence and inspire, offering a fresh perspective on African identity in the modern world.

Afrofuturist visual art also explores the intersection of mythology and modernity, creating works that are both evocative and empowering. Artists draw on traditional African symbols and narratives, reinterpreting them through modern techniques and mediums. The result is a vibrant and diverse body of work that challenges perceptions and invites viewers to explore new possibilities. These visual representations are not just about aesthetics; they are about reclaiming and redefining African identity in a global context. Through their art, these creators offer a vision of the future that is inclusive, dynamic, and deeply rooted in cultural heritage.

The cultural significance of Afrofuturism extends beyond its artistic expressions, playing a crucial role in the reclamation and celebration of African heritage. By challenging stereotypes and promoting positive representation, Afrofuturism empowers individuals to embrace their cultural identity with pride and confidence. It provides a platform for voices that have been marginalized, offering a space where African narratives are not only heard but celebrated. Afrofuturism also impacts the African diaspora's sense of identity and pride, fostering a connection to their roots that transcends geographical boundaries. Through its imaginative storytelling and bold visions of the future, Afrofuturism inspires individuals to explore their heritage and envision a world where African culture is recognized and revered. The movement encourages a reevaluation of history, offering alternative narratives that highlight the resilience and innovation of African people.

Looking to the future, Afrofuturism holds immense potential for shaping cultural narratives and artistic expressions. As the movement continues to evolve, it offers new opportunities for collaboration and exploration across various disciplines. Afrofuturism invites artists, writers, and creators from all backgrounds to engage with African mythology and culture, fostering a spirit of innovation and inclusivity. By envisioning diverse and dynamic futures, Afrofuturism challenges us to think beyond the limitations of the present, inspiring a generation of creators to push boundaries and redefine what is possible. The movement's influence extends far beyond the realms of art and literature, impacting social and political discourse by offering new ways to approach issues of identity, race, and representation. In doing so, Afrofuturism paves the way for a future where African culture is not only celebrated but central to the global narrative.

CONCLUSION

A s we journey to the end of this book, let's take a moment to revisit why we embarked on this exploration of non-Kemetic African deities and mythologies. The stories of West, Central, and Southern African pantheons are rich tapestries of culture, heritage, and spirituality. They're more than just tales of gods and goddesses; they are bridges to our past, offering insights into the values, struggles, and triumphs of our ancestors. In writing this book, the aim has been to reconnect you with these ancient narratives and help you appreciate the depth and diversity of African mythologies. While it is more of a primer than a comprehensive study, it will, hopefully, ignite sparks of curiosity and wonder.

We've traveled through vibrant landscapes of myth and legend, meeting deities like Olodumare, Shango, and Oshun from the Yoruba tradition, each with their unique stories that shape the tapestry of West African spirituality. We've delved into the tales of Nzambi a Mpungu and the water spirits of the Kongo, discovering the interconnectedness of life and the reverence for nature that defines Central African beliefs. Our journey also led us to Southern Africa, where figures like Qamata and the Rain Queen Modjadji remind us of the powerful ties between the divine and the natural world.

Throughout these chapters, key themes have emerged. The role of oral traditions in preserving culture, the importance of storytelling in teaching moral lessons, and the enduring impact of these myths on modern life have all been central to our discussion. We've seen how mythological figures not only explain natural phenomena but also serve as guardians of justice, fertility, and community harmony. The richness of African mythology is further emphasized in the trickster tales and themes of agriculture and fertility, offering timeless wisdom relevant to contemporary challenges.

What do we take away from these stories? First, a deeper understanding of African beliefs and the profound connection between people and their environment. These myths remind us of the importance of community, resilience, and the balance between humanity and nature. They challenge us to look at the world with a sense of wonder and respect, recognizing the sacred in everyday life. Moreover, they offer a source of pride and identity, a reminder that our roots are steeped in wisdom and strength.

Now, I encourage you to take this newfound knowledge and let it enrich your life. Share these stories with friends and family, rekindle traditions that may have been forgotten, and explore how these myths can inspire and guide you. Whether through participation in cultural festivals, storytelling, or simply reflecting on the lessons these deities impart, there are countless ways to keep this heritage alive.

In a world that often feels disconnected, these myths offer a profound reminder of our shared humanity and the power of stories to unite us. They teach us that despite the passage of time, the values and lessons of our ancestors remain relevant and vital. As you continue on your own path, carry these stories with you. Let them be a source of inspiration and a reminder of the rich cultural legacy that is yours to cherish.

Thank you for joining me on this journey through the pantheon of non-Kemetic African deities. It's been a privilege to walk alongside you as we explored these stories, and I hope they resonate with you as deeply as they do with me. Remember, the stories don't end here. They live on in you, waiting to be shared and celebrated. So, embrace them, learn from them, and let them be a beacon of understanding and connection in your life.

AFTERWORD

Thanks for reading my work. This project came from the heart. As a kid (who am I kidding, I'm still a kid. Just ask my wife), I loved reading about mysteries, mythologies, Gods and Legends, but I could never find a book detailing anything from Africa other than the Egyptian mythos. For a long time, I had no idea what a rich, diverse culture my ancestors lived in.

Imagine my surprise when I found out so many Gods and Legends existing in the land of my progenitors. I was astounded. Since I've delved into that amazing world, it has affected my fiction stories. Little-by-little, I've been changing tales I wrote years ago but never published. Instead of using Greek, Norse, European, or Indigenous figures and stories, I'm now using African mythos. I wish I could accurately describe how much better I feel creating with a history from which my people originated.

As this book is my first foray into this topic, I still have a lot to learn.

Thank you again. Be Well, Be Safe, and Be Blessed.

We authors thrive on feedback. It's the best way to improve our writing and engagement skills.

I would very much appreciate it if you leave a review here:

https://www.amazon.com/dp/B0DXRL89X6

If you'd like to view my other works and sign up for my mailing list, check out my website at:

https://authorcliftonbrown.com/

You can also follow me on my FB page:

https://www.facebook.com/profile.php?id=61558564643773

ABOUT THE AUTHOR

Clifton Brown is an author who draws deeply from his experiences in the U.S. Navy, weaving them into dark, evocative stories that explore the boundaries between light and shadow. With ten published short stories and a debut novel, Clifton has found writing to be a powerful way to navigate his past, honoring his service while exploring the catharsis of storytelling.

His fiction often deals with the struggle for hope amid darkness, guiding characters through love and loss in unpredictable ways. As he crafts tales of demons, extraterrestrial forces, and the supernatural, Clifton brings to life flawed, yet resilient characters, pushing them toward growth even when the path is painful. His stories delve into dark fantasy, horror, and romance, creating a space where the mysterious and the mundane collide.

Clifton's latest works include his debut novel, In The Ghost's Shadow, a dark fantasy romance about a young man with extraordinary abilities fighting alongside his love to protect Earth from a powerful, enigmatic threat. He is also the author of short stories like Dark Pink Carnations, The Z-Word, and All Hallows Snipe Hunt, each blending elements of the uncanny with human struggle and desire. These works, published by Wicked Shadow Press, continue to showcase his penchant for dark fiction—stories where heroes must confront monstrous forces, both within and without, to emerge into whatever light they can find.

With an affinity for the weird and the wondrous, Clifton enjoys creating worlds where danger is ever-present, but love and resilience still shine through, however unexpectedly.

REFERENCES

Re-Afurakanising Kemet: Re-Membering the ... https://www.modernghana.com/news/1228020/re-afurakanising-kemet-re-membering-the-dismember.html

A Comparative Study of 'Genesis' Stories Across Cultures https://www.researchgate.net/publication/379333886_A_Comparative_Study_of_'Genesis'_Stories_Across_Cultures

Griot | West African, Oral Tradition, Storyteller https://www.britannica.com/art/griot

African Mythology: History and Modern-Day Relevance https://www.africarebirth.com/african-mythology-history-and-modern-day-relevance/

Olodumare: The Supreme Creator in Nigerian Mythology - Oriire https://www.oriire.com/article/olodumare-the-supreme-creator-in-nigerian-mythology#:~:text=The%20Yoruba%20myth%20of%20creation%20tells%20the%20story%20of%20how,was%20only%20darkness%20and%20silence.

Shango | Yoruba God of Thunder, Lightning & Justice https://www.britannica.com/topic/Shango

Oshun | Yoruba Goddess of Love, Fertility & Abundance https://www.britannica.com/topic/Oshun#:~:text=Every%20year%20Oshun%20devotees%20and,festival%20is%20centred%20on%20Oshun.

Eshu | African God, Trickster, Orisha - Britannica https://www.britannica.com/topic/Eshu#:~:text=Eshu%2C%20trickster%20god%20of%20the,sacrifices%20and%20divining%20the%20future.

Nzambi a Mpungu https://en.wikipedia.org/wiki/Nzambi_a_Mpungu

Simbi: The Water and Nature Spirit in African Kongo ... https://panafrocore.com/2024/03/11/simbi-the-water-and-nature-spirit-in-african-kongo-spirituality-and-hoodoo/

Kimpa   Vita: The   unity   prophet
https://www.dw.com/en/kimpa-vita-the-unity-prophet/a-53546026

Mbokomu   -   Womanifest   Your   Power   with   Abiola
https://womanifesting.com/african-goddess-cards/mbokomu/

Qamata https://en.wikipedia.org/wiki/Qamata

Unkulunkulu : The Creator God https://mythlok.com/unkulunkulu/

Rain Queen https://en.wikipedia.org/wiki/Rain_Queen

THIXO - the Xhosa God of Creation (African mythology)
https://www.godchecker.com/african-mythology/THIXO/

Olodumare: The Supreme Creator in Nigerian Mythology - Oriire
https://www.oriire.com/article/olodumare-the-supreme-creator-in-nigerian-mythology
#:~:text=The%20Yoruba%20myth%20of%20creation%20tells%20the%20story%20of%2
0how,was%20only%20darkness%20and%20silence.

Nzambi a Mpungu https://en.wikipedia.org/wiki/Nzambi_a_Mpungu

Zulu   Creation   Myth | African   Tribal   Folktales
https://www.gateway-africa.com/stories/Zulu_Creation_Myth.html

ON   THE   CONCEPT   OF   CREATION   IN   ...
https://www.ajol.info/index.php/og/article/view/217834/205441

Eshu | African God, Trickster, Orisha https://www.britannica.com/topic/Eshu

Ashanti   of   Ghana: How   Spider   Obtained   Sky-God's   Stories
https://wilderutopia.com/traditions/myth/ashanti-of-ghana-how-spider-obtained-the-s
ky-gods-stories/

LEGBA - Guardian of the Crossroads - National Park Service
https://www.nps.gov/afbg/learn/historyculture/legba.htm#:~:text=Legba%20represen
ts%20a%20West%20African,in%20Haiti%20as%20Papa%20Legba.

98.02.04: Three African Trickster Myths/Tales -- Primary Style
https://teachersinstitute.yale.edu/curriculum/units/1998/2/98.02.04/3

Oshun | Yoruba Goddess of Love, Fertility & Abundance
https://www.britannica.com/topic/Oshun#:~:text=Oshun%20is%20commonly%20cal
led%20the,vanity%2C%20jealousy%2C%20and%20spite.

Mbokomu (deity) https://en.wikipedia.org/wiki/Mbokomu_(deity)

The   myth,   the   place,   the   Queen   –   Queen   Modjadji
https://www.dstv.com/mzansimagic/en-za/news/the-myth-the-place-the-queen-queen-
modjadji

Asase Yaa : The Earth Goddess https://mythlok.com/asase-yaa/

THE   YORUBA   BELIEF   IN   LIFE   AFTER   DEATH
https://www.obafemio.com/uploads/5/1/4/2/5142021/dopamu-lifeafter_death.pdf

Kongo   Cosmogram   -   Levi   Jordan   Plantation
http://www.webarchaeology.com/html/kongocos.htm

The Zulu People - Uvelaphi https://www.uvelaphi.co.za/cultures/zulu

Remembering   Our   Ancestors: A   Legacy   of   African   Spirituality
https://medium.com/@feliciamlittle/remembering-our-ancestors-a-legacy-of-african-spirituality-85eb27cace1a

The   Tokoloshe: Mythology   and   Modern   Trauma
https://viewfromthedark.ca/2019/02/17/the-tokoloshe-mythology-and-modern-trauma/

Mami Wata: Arts for Water Spirits in Africa and its Diasporas
https://africa.si.edu/exhibits/mamiwata/intro.html

Grootslang https://en.wikipedia.org/wiki/Grootslang

Adze   (folklore)   -   Wikipedia
https://en.wikipedia.org/wiki/Adze_(folklore)#:~:text=The%20adze%20is%20a%20vampiric,the%20power%20to%20possess%20humans.

Anansi   Stories: From   West   Africa   to   the   Caribbean
https://orijinculture.com/community/anansi-stories-west-africa-caribbean/

Anansi https://en.wikipedia.org/wiki/Anansi

The   Lion's   Whiskers: An   Ethiopian   Folktale
https://globalschoollibrary.wordpress.com/2016/05/10/the-lions-whiskers-an-ethiopian-folktale/

The   three   brothers   and   the   pot   of   porridge
http://www.allfolktales.com/wafrica/three_brothers_and_porridge.php

Ogun: The   Warrior   and   Blacksmith   of   Yoruba   Mythology
https://arsgoetiademons.com/blogs/spirits-deities/ogun-the-warrior-and-blacksmith-of-yoruba-mythology?srsltid=AfmBOoo5mJrgBzzmd1wXGOKAT0Rtp5UOfPLZl1AFA8C03M3yoPwYQIvf

Yemoja - Wikipedia https://en.wikipedia.org/wiki/Yem%E1%BB%8Dja

Queen   Nzinga   (1583-1663)   •
https://www.blackpast.org/global-african-history/queen-nzinga-1583-1663/

Haile Selassie I | Biography, Rastafarian, Wife, Death, & Facts
https://www.britannica.com/biography/Haile-Selassie-I#:~:text=As%20emperor%20of
%20Ethiopia%20(1930,African%20race%20by%20many%20Rastas.

The Proliferation of Yorùbá Religion in the Atlantic during ...
https://journals.flvc.org/ysr/article/view/132800

Syncretism and Cognition: African and European Religious ...
https://academic.oup.com/book/44171/chapter/372391277

Afrofuturism Then and Now | Pulitzer Center
https://1619education.org/builder/lesson/afrofuturism-then-and-now

Òrìṣà Devotion as World Religion https://uwpress.wisc.edu/books/2441.htm

An Evening With Sona Jobarteh https://www.artidea.org/VLE2024

The Ancient Craft of Jaliyaa:
https://babathestoryteller.com/the-ancient-craft-of-jaliyaa/

The Hand of Nzambi: An Ethnographic Study of Palo Mayombe Nkisi Malongo
Across the Atlantic https://original-ufdc.uflib.ufl.edu/UFE0058792/00001

This African Creation Myth Highlights The Liberating Power Of Forgiveness
https://www.pushblackspirit.com/this-african-creation-myth-highlights-the-liberating-
power-of-forgiveness/

The Moral of Tortoise and Hare Fable: U.S.
vs. African Version By: Author Lillie Marshall
https://www.aroundtheworldl.com/unity-and-help-the-lesson-of-the-tortoise/

www.ingramcontent.com/pod-product-compliance
Lightning Source LLC
Chambersburg PA
CBHW022118280326
41933CB00007B/437